TRANSMONTANUS 21

Gardens Aflame

Series Editor: Terry Glavin

Published by New Star Books

Other books in the Transmontanus series

Gardens Aflame

GARRY OAK MEADOWS OF BC'S SOUTH COAST

Maleea Acker

TRANSMONTANUS I NEW STAR BOOKS VANCOUVER

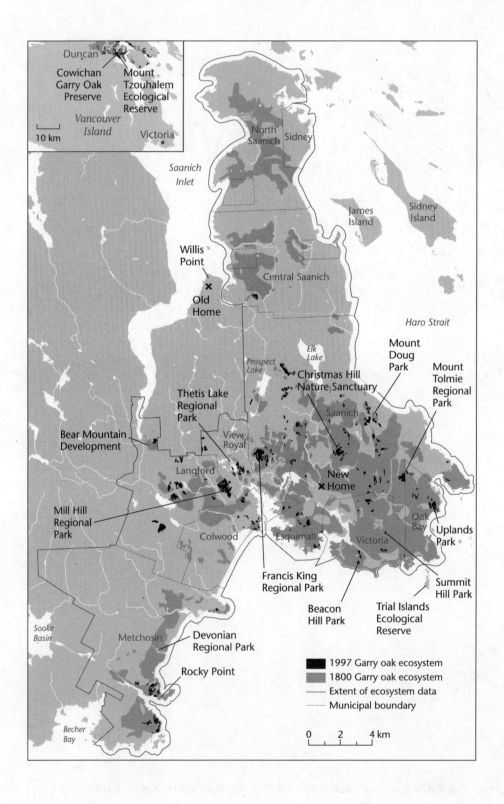

Duncan

Cowichan
Garry Oak
Preserve

Mount
Tzouhalem
Ecological
Reserve

*Vancouver
Island*

10 km

Victoria

*Saanich
Inlet*

North
Saanich

Sidney

James
Island

Sidney
Island

Willis
Point

✕
Old
Home

Central Saanich

Haro Strait

*Elk
Lake*

*Prospect
Lake*

Mount
Doug
Park

Mount
Tolmie
Regional
Park

Christmas Hill
Nature Sanctuary

Thetis Lake
Regional
Park

Saanich

View
Royal

Bear Mountain
Development

Langford

✕
New
Home

Mill Hill
Regional
Park

Colwood

Esquimalt

Victoria

Oak
Bay

Uplands
Park

Francis King
Regional Park

Summit
Hill Park

Beacon
Hill Park

Trial Islands
Ecological
Reserve

*Sooke
Basin*

Metchosin

Devonian
Regional Park

Rocky Point

*Becher
Bay*

■ 1997 Garry oak ecosystem
■ 1800 Garry oak ecosystem
— Extent of ecosystem data
⋯ Municipal boundary

0   2   4 km

Contents

Preface

Throughout history, humans have turned to the natural world for solace and healing. In both wilderness and gardens, we find sanctuary. Our relationship to nature, however, is complicated. In wilderness, we escape our own history, are relieved of the clamor of human existence. We cannot possess the wild. We face the unsettling reality of being but one of the many creatures on this earth. The world goes on very fluidly and beautifully without philosophy, tractors or stock exchanges. As Robert Pogue Harrison writes in *Forests*, "to be human means to be always and already outside of the forest's inclusion." Our attempts to interact with or translate the wild are full of the longing that stems from our sense that we are outsiders.

In gardens, we are free to cultivate our own particular sense of beauty, meaning and wonder, to work a parcel of the earth until it looks and acts, more or less, as we would wish. But our attempts to recreate paradise through cultivation are also fraught with difficulty. Restlessness, an impulse to control, a misguided sense of the value of cultivation's work — all these contend with the peace and the ethic of care that tending fosters. While gardens provide solace, they are often also a lesson in patience, humility and relinquishment.

A Garry oak meadow is full with wild flora and fauna, but exists only because of thousands of years of careful cultivation by a society now dispossessed. It is a contested space, and now it is endangered, the project of thousands who work for its protection. Today, our appetite for its charms is matched by the damage to it we have done. As such, it is an ideal microcosm for examining the aesthetic, ethical and economic preoccupations that have dogged our species. Ultimately, a Garry oak meadow can show us how to live in the world.

Home

*As it is now, it is an imposing semi-architectural
experience, whose rooms are not like rooms at all,
but high narrow places found and then embellished
with vegetable scribbling.*

— ROBERT HARBISON, *Eccentric Spaces*

To experience the architectural room of a Garry oak meadow is
to undertake a journey, one which begins by stepping backward,
rather than forward. If we begin with a European understanding of
cultivation, we must reimagine a garden without furrows, plough,
or the seeds brought from the old world; supposing it a wilderness, we must learn to recognize the signs of human involvement,
which arranged this wilderness and made its *vegetable scribbling*
into *a semi-architectural experience* that is anything but simply
wild.

By taking this journey, we find a landscape of complexity and
diversity as yet uncharted; a world created but unrepeatable; a
manner of living where form, function, aesthetics and spiritual
importance interweave back through thousands of years of history. With each step back, the view of the meadows alters, and
understanding — of what it is to be human, to be wild, and to live
intertwined with the world — enlarges and grows more rich.

*

The journey of this book is also the arc of a personal migration, which took me, sometimes willingly, sometimes very much against my will, from one distinct Vancouver Island landscape to another. A long-time amateur gardener and ecosystem restorationist, I had spent the previous seven years besotted by, and frustrated with, the shadowed, thin-soiled Douglas fir and arbutus ecosystem that surrounded my home in the unincorporated community of Willis Point, on southern Vancouver Island. It was a north slope forest, and after many failed farming attempts — the land's one mossy clearing provided inadequate in light even for lettuce, and a bear ate the tomatoes I grew in the Ministry of Highways road allowance ditch — I surrendered and turned my efforts to the resuscitation of calypso orchids, deer ferns and conifers. A green oasis flourished — a coastal forest identical to those I was raised in, the light muted by black branches of firs and wide leaves of Arbutus rather than showcased by a cathedral sky.

Then, a week after I signed the contract to write this book, my marriage ended. I began a nomadic period, moving every two to three weeks to house-sits or apartments of friends and forcing myself to rediscover the island's landscapes and its southern city by bike and by foot. By fall, I found myself in a miniature 1940s house, in a nearly treeless Saanich neighbourhood. My former home and its forest were so beloved to me I used to feel my chest relax every time I turned onto our long road. I had no idea where I was, what I wanted or how I had arrived. To throw myself into the realm of Garry oak meadows — sunlit grassland ecosystems full of wildflowers and gnarled trees — was a way of putting to rest my great attachment to the darker, acidic forest of coastal Douglas fir; it prevented complete heartbreak; it got me through.

This journey also echoes the larger story of a lost southeastern Vancouver Island, where evidence of a long and stable history has been displaced by today's fragmented one. European settlement from the 1860s to the turn of the century destroyed nearly all of Vancouver Island's deep-soil Garry oak meadows. Many of the shallow-soil upland sites, however, though threatened by invasive species such as English ivy and Scotch broom, remained untouched by housing tracts and other development. If no longer managed by aboriginal agriculture or fire, they were at least, more or less, left to their own devices.

As recently as the 1970s, it was still possible for boat builders Allan and Sherrie Farrell to beach an old dory at the shoreline of one of Lasqueti Island's rocky oak meadows and build a sailboat, using hand tools and driftwood and gathering food from the shore and fields for their meals. Oaks and arbutus grew over the still coves and turquoise bays, along foreshores strewn with the middens from thousands of years of First Nations food gathering and feasting.

Dionysio Provincial Park, Galiano Island.

Today, where once there were meadows, there are now developments with names like Green Oaks, Oak Glen and Meadow Haven. The results of this housing boom can be seen on Christmas Hill in Victoria, and Mount Tzouhalem outside of Duncan, where giant homes crawl up the slopes to the very edges of each protected Garry oak area. Much of the native ecosystem in these areas was sacrificed in exchange for protection of the most ecologically important parcels. The Garry Oak Ecosystem Recovery Team (GOERT) estimates that between one and five percent of original Garry oak ecosystems now remain on the southwest coast of Canada; less than one percent is deemed intact. Where once there were unbroken waves of blue camas fields, stretching from the cliffs of Clover Point up through Rockland, Hillside and Swan Lake, there are now only remnants. Beacon Hill, Uplands Park, the Matson Conservation Lands and Anderson Hill are some of these vestiges. Otherwise, most remaining oaks sit in cultivated yards of European grasses. The unevenly dividing bark of these trees, reaching far above the houses, remains a welcome grey-brown against winter blue sky. These oaks — though they are part of a biological refugia, as biologist Briony Penn and ethno-botanist Nancy Turner argue — are just remnants of the entire ecosystem, and are too often strangled by invasive species, threatened by development, drought or overgrowth by Douglas fir and other species.

The conservation agencies, restoration experts and countless volunteers across the south island that pull broom, remove ivy, and plant camas and young oaks also cherish Garry oak ecosystems. The reverence they show is this book's common thread. It is deeply satisfying to return to a site year after year as a volunteer and see its revival. Mostly, however, people just love being in the meadows. They are the thing that springs to mind when people are asked to describe a quintessential southern Vancouver Island landscape. They represent us; they sustain us, as they did past generations of First Nations; they continue to be one of our sacred spaces.

In late 2011, the Garry Oak Ecosystems Recovery Team published a stunning compendium of research on BC's south coast meadows; the May 2011 issue of the journal *Northwest Science* was dedicated entirely to prairie and oak woodlands in Washington, Oregon and British Columbia. It is not the intent of this book to reproduce that valuable work, but rather to explore what the meadows originally represented: gardens that housed and protected a food source, that provided us with solace and fulfilling work, that still serve as a storehouse of biological diversity, and that remain, in remnants, beautiful spaces that mend our hearts and minds.

Respite Space, Contested Space

A Garry oak meadow is a garden. Managed intricately by First Nations families and communities for centuries before Europe-

ans arrived, the open, arching spaces embodied both function
and form. They were, as Nancy Turner and fellow ethnographer
Brenda Beckwith have documented, constructed landscapes, created and managed through use of fire and species selection, in
order to enhance their productivity and maintain their structure.
But utilitarian use of the meadows was not their only value. The
meadows also acted as an exterior interior, a meeting place for the
creation of peace treaties between nations or tribes. They held
those who attended their leafy rooms in an intimate but spacious
embrace.

*Camas
in bloom,
Uplands Park.*

For First Nations, this embrace also extended through to life on
the other side. As humans, we place our dead in those landscapes
that are most dear, that have import. From the fields of Flanders to
small Our Lady of the Assumption Church on a hill above Saanich
Inlet, our burial sites reveal our notions of beauty, of vista, openness and spiritual power. Coastal Salish burial mounds and cairns
litter Garry oak meadows across the south island: on Metchosin's
Rocky Point, in Uplands Park (where they were used by early surveyors as convenient markers), at Beacon Hill, and at many other

locations on the south island. Whatever the arrangement of stones might mean, whatever facet of family or village identity was being expressed, the fact remains that they chose an oak-and-camas landscape — the garden they also cultivated for food — in which to place and harbour their beloved. Gardens, as philosopher Robert Harbison writes in *Eccentric Spaces*, "always mean something else, man absolutely uses one thing to say another."

> Trees, bushes, and slopes show us closeness, separation, dependence, arrest, depression, exultation. Rarely even in dreams can a person get such a sense of traversing years in a jump, surmounting obstacles with a few sloping steps, looking back on the past with a turn of the head.

On one hand, respite space. On the other, contested space. Captain James Cook first visited the shores of Vancouver Island in 1778, sailing into Nootka Sound aboard the *Resolution*. But the land of Vancouver Island was not deeded to the Hudson's Bay *Summit Park,* Company until almost 100 years later, when the village of Camo-
Victoria. sack, later renamed Victoria, was founded in 1849 by Sir James

Douglas. The site was chosen for a settlement primarily because of the almost six square miles of Garry oak meadows that surrounded the harbour. Though Esquimalt's harbour was larger and Sooke Harbour was closer to the open Pacific, their rocky aspect and Sooke's inclement weather did not appeal to explorers who needed land for food production. In a letter to James Hargrave in 1843, Sir James Douglas described the Victoria area as akin to the finest pleasure grounds in Europe. "The place itself appears a perfect 'Eden' in the midst of the dreary wilderness of the North ... one might be pardoned for supposing it had dropped from the clouds into its present position."

According to philosopher Robert Pogue Harrison, in his work *Gardens*, we have historically understood two visions of Eden. The first was a walled garden — described by Epicurus as peaceful, full of repose and lacking in toil. To rest in contented peace, with no need to improve one's surroundings, was the original idea of Eden. As human beings became more mobile, however, and began the takeover of foreign lands, we also became less satisfied with tranquility as an adequate vision of paradise. Gone, long before Douglas's time, was our sense that our every desire might be satisfied there; it was replaced by a craving "to 'make' a *paradiso terrestre*." Even if the place we arrive at reminds us of the lost garden, as did Garry oak meadows for Douglas, we continue to suffer, Harrison writes, from a perpetual dissatisfaction.

> The craving for more life engenders from its own dynamism the myth that there is a place where all desires are gratified, all pain is abolished, the curse of Adam is overcome, and human beings have no other responsibility than to be unfettered consumers of goods, entertainment, information and pleasures.

The consequence of both this striving and our dissatisfaction has been an unending sense of dislocation. Through endless consumption, satisfaction remains just out of reach. Always searching for more, Harrison writes, "we find ourselves in the paradoxical situation of seeking to re-create Eden by ravaging the garden itself."

James Douglas' description of the meadows as an Eden is disturbing for the irony of its limited vision. He describes a cultivated landscape — Garry oak meadows that stretched across the south

Uplands area oak landscape, ca. *1890s, showing burial cairns and encroaching Garry oak into aboriginally maintained savannah. Collection of George Harvey.* CITY OF VICTORIA ARCHIVES, PHOTO M08548

island — as a wilderness. Douglas recognized the landscape he arrived at as akin to the English countryside — pastoral, with a pleasure-garden look. He did not make the imaginative leap, however, from recognition of similarity to acknowledgement or understanding of this familiar landscape as "managed." The idea of a cultivated landscape that did not bear obvious scars of man was inconceivable. According to Nancy Turner, even a more enlightened ethnographer such as Franz Boas, "despite his fierce debunking disposition on many anthropological questions — chose to reiterate rather than to challenge European explorers' claims on this point." His disinclination, writes Turner in *Keeping it Living,* may have been because Boas "equated 'agriculture' with the cultivation of a small range of domesticated crops....Boas was reluctant to term patterns of plant management based on vegetative transplanting and use of perennial species as true 'cultivation.' "

The portrayal of Coast Salish and other Northwest Coast First Nations societies as primarily hunter-gatherer rather than agricultural was key to legitimizing the European occupation of managed Garry oak meadows, and set the stage for meadows' new status as contested spaces. In 1868, Gilbert Malcom Sproat, Commissioner on the Joint Committee on Indian Reserves, asserted that "we might justify our occupation of Vancouver Island by the fact of all the land lying waste without prospect of improvement." Plants such as camas and riceroot, which First Nations identified when asked what their forefathers had cultivated in "unimproved" areas, were not recognized as cultivars by the commission. "Most such claims were summarily denied unless the sites happened to coincide with the location of a village fishing station," Turner wrote. As such, "most terrestrial sites — including almost all sites where traditional plant-management practices still endured — fell out of Aboriginal control."

The problem was compounded as up to 90 percent of First Nations coastal populations, according to some estimates, died from disease epidemics of smallpox, tuberculosis and flu that spread from the 1780s until the late 1800s. As a result, Garry oak meadows ceased to be managed — by fire or cultivation — as they had been for millennia. Thus Europeans that immigrated to the island found a landscape that was largely abandoned; the meadows they encountered were in the early stages of neglect. After disease swept the land, there were no longer adequate First Nation populations left to harvest, manage and cultivate the meadows. The Reserves system further restricted traditional management practices. Finally, settlers affected the meadows by encouraging fire suppression, high-intensity agriculture using European plants and division of land. As European descendants 'tamed' the south island's deep-soil meadows, they also created farms and urban gardens with plants from the world they had left behind, displacing local species.

The buildings and enclosures we have created since Douglas's landing — places of worship, fenced farms, cemeteries and homes — and the contested spaces we choose to create them in have become testament to the power we wish to hold. It is no accident that the most valuable lands in greater Victoria also tend to be those with the greatest concentration of oaks. In today's supermarket age, remaining shallow-soil meadows, with their lack of soil but pleasing views and southern aspect, have become our newly contested spaces. Thus, to walk into a Garry oak meadow is to walk into a version of Eden, defined by spiritual connection and aesthetic pleasure; it is also a space defined by trade and monetary value — a space that has been both earned and bought.

There is a myth about camas told by the Okanagan and Colville tribes. Blue Flower, of the Kalispel peoples, came over the mountains to marry one of three brothers from the Okanagan. The three suitors quarreled, and in response, Blue Flower took her basket of camas bulbs and threw them back over the ridge to the Kalispel lands. She wanted no camas to grow in the valley of the Okanagan people. This was her last act before singing her power song and turning herself to stone. She was the food that should never be fought over; this flower of sustenance and peace did not belong with them.

The story remains significant today, as does the conclusion to Blue Flower's second life as a wishing stone. First Nations and European settlers visited the stone for hundreds of years; gifts were left at its side, as even the smallest was said to bring good luck. It guarded the ridge between the Okanagan and the Kalispel valleys, in Northeastern Washington. That is, until a prospector heard that there was treasure buried under the stone and destroyed it, in 1900, with dynamite.

Meadows

It was the third-coldest spring ever recorded on the west coast of Canada. Farmers started out in March a little worried, then there was an early April snowfall and temperatures still didn't rise. By May, we were four weeks behind normal growing season and more than six degrees below normal in temperatures. This also meant an incredibly late bloom for Garry oak meadows. At May's end, camas was just coming to peak bloom in many locations. Cold winds kept the oak trees from unfurling until the middle of the month. The cold temperatures also meant a setback for many of the bees and other insects normally out in full force by May. Matt Fairburns, volunteer warden for Trial Island Ecological Reserve, told me he had seen a precipitous drop in the populations of early-spring annuals, including rare species like white meconella, Idaho scalepod and Macoun's meadowfoam. Maybe, he mused, next year we will see the reverse. In the meantime, we struggled through a season that tested even the most patient, and it was mid June before true warmth arrived.

Garry oaks are the only oak native to British Columbia. They were named by David Douglas, a botanist who worked with Nicholas Garry, a deputy governor of the Hudson's Bay Company for whom Douglas developed a fondness. The oaks, which are called Oregon white oak south of the border, inhabit the northern end of their range on the south coast of Canada, and can be found on the

*Garry oak
tree bark.*

east coast of Vancouver Island from Victoria to Courtney, and in
two isolated patches at Yale and Sumas Mountain in BC's Fraser
Valley; eastward, they spread to the Cascades and follow warm,
dry habitats through Tacoma and the Willamette and Umpqua
valleys to northern California. The further south one travels, the
more Garry oaks are displaced by other native California oak species such as the California black oak and, in very dry sites, by the
canyon oak.

Before European contact, Garry oak meadows covered much
of southern Vancouver Island. According to the Garry Oak Ecosystems Recovery Team, as of 2006, coverage of the ecosystem
had been reduced to 1,589 hectares from 15,249 hectares. Deep-
soil meadows have suffered an even more precipitous drop; from
12,009 hectares pre-European settlement to 175 hectares in 2006.

Garry oak communities are unusual in that they harbour a wide
range of sub-habitats, where vernal pools, dry rocky outcrops,
grasslands, coastal bluffs and deep-soil woodlands can be found.
As such, an amazing variety of insects, amphibians, lizards, birds
and mammals are associated with the ecosystem. There are, for
example, several species of native bees in oak meadows that are
specialist pollinators, visiting only one species or genus of plant
and thus providing a perfect, though vulnerable, pollination relationship. New species of mushroom and moss, and isolated group-

ings of plants previously thought to be extirpated are still being discovered today in the meadows, mostly in high, rocky, thin soiled areas. The ecosystem is home to more plant species than any other terrestrial ecosystem in coastal British Columbia. The meadows house 60 percent of the province's endangered or at-risk listed species.

Garry oaks ecosystems are so well adapted to the mild winters and dry summers of our region that their dormancy period takes place during the summer, rather than through the winter, as with other deciduous species. Indeed, it is the specific climate and geography of Vancouver Island and the Gulf Islands that allows the ecosystem to thrive. Once fall rains arrive, roots begin growing again and bulbs such as camas, the mature examples of which can be found more than a foot under the soil surface, begin sending out their leaf stalks for the following spring's bloom. Unlike the acidic soil conditions of coastal Douglas fir, hemlock and cedar forests, Garry oak meadows build rich, black, loamy soil through the yearly growth and decomposition of grasses and flowers. In lowland areas, this can translate into incredibly fertile conditions. Good soil, combined with a tendency to inhabit warm, dry, sunny areas, have made Garry oak ecosystems the primary site for agricultural and residential development for the past 150 years. This alone has contributed much to their current status as an endangered ecosystem.

Garry oak trees themselves are instantly recognizable, even to those not botanically inclined. Their bark is pitted and corrugated, their branches are knotted, blackish-grey and bare in winter; come spring they grow hazy with fawn-coloured buds; as they leaf out, their flame-hued leaves quickly turn pale green, then dark and leathery, with velvet, moss-green undersides in summer. The arched spaces the oaks etch overhead in a meadow can feel cathedral-like.

In urban Greater Victoria, oaks themselves are now often the only remaining species from their ecosystem. They grow out of lawns, they sprout from golf courses, they stand three times the size of city trees on boulevards in Saanich, Victoria and Oak Bay. Often over-watered in summer on private property, they also suffer from drought in public spaces where pavement or short-cut grass allow parching of the earth.

FEBRUARY 5, 2011: PLAYFAIR PARK, SAANICH

My dog, Maisie, and I step out of the car at Playfair Park into the pouring rain of a Saturday afternoon. My first visit to the groves this year. She immediately climbs back in the car and looks at me ruefully, as if to say, "You really want to go for a walk in this?" We slip across the fields and circle the oaks, crossing over the green grass of winter and the mud of the rains. It's completely windless and devoid of movement. I can hear the traffic from the streets below. The sky seems to hover just above our heads. The trees are like corrugated imitations of themselves. As if we have arrived on the set of a stage play, the wires ready to pull each tree, each rock back up into the flyway at a moment's notice. At the same time, like a play, the landscape is completely itself. Without the riot of bloom and colour, blue sky and birdsong to distract, I can see the meadow as it is, unvarnished, without garland, staring me straight in the eye. We scramble over the trail and double back. The rain falls harder. Maisie looks at me and makes a run for the car. I follow.

Types of Garry Oak Ecosystems

Once European populations began to arrive, Vancouver Island was surveyed (between 1859 and 1874) in order to determine potentially productive lands. Though not ecosystem maps, these surveys are still useful for the categories of woodland they describe. Using bearing trees and survey posts, surveyors counted the number and type of "stems" or trees in an area. In 1859 in the Cowichan Valley, for instance, more than 50 percent of the surveyed land was comprised of what surveyors called Prairie, Plains or Open Woods, which were defined, respectively, as having 8, 61 or 227 stems per hectare. The plains were described in 1859 by surveyor Oliver Wells, of the Shawnigan District, as "land of the best quality, open, and little wood upon it, which usually grows in clumps with an occasional isolated tree. The picturesque effect being very similar to that of an extensive cultivated park." Historical photos in the Uplands area of Victoria show open grasslands: light-filled spaces, with widely spaced trees and fields of mosses, short, bunching grasses such as Roemer's fescue and a host of wildflowers.

Researcher Darcy Mathews describes the original oak parkland that First Nations managed as almost completely devoid of any trees, save the occasional large Douglas fir or Garry oak. With the arrival of Europeans, agricultural and urban development claimed most of southeastern Vancouver Island. What was not claimed has been subjected to intense changes in management. Fire suppression, invasive species and grazing all take their toll on native species. Introduced insects such as the jumping gall wasp and oak-leaf Phylloxera scorch the leaves of oaks, inhibiting their ability to photosynthesize. More recently, there have also been dramatic decreases in species that either spread acorns (such as the Steller's jay) or inhibit the growth of competing tree and brush species through browsing (such as black-tailed deer and Roosevelt elk). In a second round of land surveying, completed in 2007, populations of Garry oak trees grew dramatically from 1874 records on Salt Spring Island and in the Cowichan Valley. Lack of fire is thought to have been the primary cause of this increase.

Garry oak meadows can be found in a variety of situations on BC's south coast, including dry, semi-dry and wet conditions. Oaks such as those found at Mill Hill or Mount Douglas grow in poor soils over bedrock and develop low to the ground, often resembling bushes rather than trees. Tall Oregon grape is often present, along with a variety of drought-resistant herbs and grasses, and amphibians such as the alligator lizard. These meadows are the most frequently found ecosystem remnant on the south coast of Vancouver Island. In summer, the higher bluffs turn golden and parched. Christmas Hill, Gonzales Hill, Anderson Hill and Mount Tolmie have all seen houses encroach up to the edges of each park; a majority date from the 1960s, and many were built in just the last 20 years. Shallow meadows provide the perfect combination of spectacular vista and hollowed, protected nook. They are both intimate and vast.

As land begins to level off and soils deepen, a greater variety of understory plants can be supported. These areas drain to drought conditions by late summer but still support some shrubby plants. Oak trees tend to be taller than on drier slopes and camas is prominent in spring. As the terrain continues to level and groundwater increases, oaks thrive in the deep-soiled, rambling ecosystems found in Victoria's Beacon Hill Park, and Duncan's Cowichan Garry Oak Preserve and Quamichan Reserve. Oaks in these meadows, due to excellent soil and moisture conditions, attain a stately, broad stature, with a regular crown and straight trunks that often reach more than twenty-five metres in height. If not subject to burning, these sites are easily overtaken with a shrubby understory of common snowberry, ocean spray and Nootka rose. As the meadows were excellent camas harvesting sites, many still bear the remnants of cooking pit depressions, burial cairns and village sites. Of the deep-soil meadows that once covered the Cowichan Valley, Blenkinsop Valley, parts of the Saanich Peninsula, Metchosin, Esquimalt, Colwood, Victoria and many other areas in between, almost nothing remains intact. A few examples can still be seen today at the Cowichan Preserve, in a stand in Beacon Hill Park and at Metchosin's Rocky Point Department of National Defence lands.

Trial Island open meadows of camas, historically maintained by First Nations people.

Species

Garry oak ecosystems contain more than 694 species of plant, including more than 100 species identified as at risk by the Com-

mittee on the Status of Endangered Wildlife in Canada. The listed species inventory in Garry oak ecosystems as of 2011 included 7 reptile species, 7 amphibian species, 104 birds and 33 mammals. The meadows also support 800 species of insects, with 140 feeding on the oaks themselves. Sixty-six vascular plants, 3 mosses, 1 earthworm, 13 butterflies and 11 other insects are listed as at risk. Vertebrates at risk include 2 reptiles, 14 birds and 3 mammals. (Plants mentioned in this book appear in the appendix.)

Garry Oak (Quercus garryana)

The Garry oak is BC's only native deciduous oak. The bark, whiteish-grey and black, runs in vertical lines along the trunk. In high winds the tree tends to crack rather than bend in the wind; the hollows left by shed branches support cavity nesting birds — nuthatches, wrens, woodpeckers, bluebirds and swallows. Their acorns serve as a primary food source for many species and may have been carried north by First Nations, aiding in their historical spread up the coast. Though Garry oak acorns are said to have been eaten occasionally by Coast Salish, they took immense amounts of cooking and preparation to rid them of their bitter taste, and so were not cultivated specifically for food. The wood itself, writes Nancy Turner in *Food Plants of Coastal First Peoples*, was often used for camas digging sticks and combs. When barelimbed in winter, the trees appear to many as witch-like, clawed, ever dividing, with next year's buds visible as small, brownish-grey pearls at the end of their knobby branches. They are both stately and fragile, dropping twigs incessantly through the year and driving those who love the look of a manicured lawn a little mad.

Garry oaks are a key species in the meadows, but their inability to self-perpetuate in most coastal habitats, where they are out-competed by other native trees, such as Douglas fir and bigleaf maple, made the survival of open oak woodlands dependent on First Nations' use of fire, used up and down the coast as a cultivation technique. Fire suppression was one of the most important factors in the ecosystem's disappearance, rating far above logging, grazing or climate change. Before the arrival of Europeans, fires, both naturally occurring and set by First Nations, rolled through Garry oak meadow ecosystems at three- to five-year intervals: a process the Cowichan call "sweetening the ground." Fire maintained the open understory of a meadow, keeping woody shrubs and oaks to a minimum. The resulting grassland, as Turner documented, was a better habitat for wildflowers and thus resulted in higher camas yields for First Nations. Fire let in sunlight, added nutrients to the soil and stimulated the germination of seeds. If there is a conservation stewardship tool that makes the most dramatic positive difference to the health of Garry oak ecosystems, it may be fire. It has also, however, been the most difficult tool to reintroduce in the meadows, mainly because of restrictions on burning and fear that fires will grow to uncontrollable sizes, threatening residences and farms. Growing sprawl in rural areas means a smaller buffer between wild areas and human-inhabited ones.

A Garry oak grove's history can also be estimated by each tree's position in a meadow. When we see a circle of oak trees in a field, says Fred Hook, Natural Areas technician with Victoria Parks, the centre of the circle they form likely indicates the location of a larger, long disappeared oak. The original tree suckers out from the living roots in a ring around the trunk. The central tree eventually dies; the children continue. This next generation of oaks are related by gene to one another, in the way that a whole grove of trembling aspen in Alberta can be a part of one organism. With aspen, the relation is obvious come spring and fall, when trees belonging to the same root system green up and turn colour at exactly the same time. With Garry oaks, the connection was not clear until genetic testing was done. Tests have shown that two oaks hundreds of feet apart can share the exact same makeup — they are essentially part of one tree, their root systems a vestige of or an actual connection to a common parent trunk.

Camas (Camassia quamash and Camassia leichtlinii)

Great camas and common camas lilies blanket many Garry oak meadows in mid-spring. Great camas is larger and less common; its tepals (a form of petal) twist together after flowering to protect the fruit. Camas leaves emerge in March: thick, almost succulent-like. The stem includes five or more indigo flowers with yolk-yellow stamens. They have no scent. In full bloom they have been compared to a blue lake, so thick can be their carpet. These days, we are lucky to see patches of them, scattered throughout the Cowichan or Mount Tzouhalem Preserves, or in small hollows at Uplands Park, the Matson Lands or Devonian Regional Park. Coast Salish First Nations have, historically, had an incredibly intimate relationship with camas. The late Patricia Boyle, who created an exquisite native plant garden on Gonzales Bay in Oak Bay, wrote, "Every time I plant camas I think of its links to all the generations of women who tended and harvested camas bulbs for food on Vancouver Island." Nancy Turner has amassed incredible oral histories regarding the plant, and many have called camas one of the "valuables of the earth," which, along with other flowers, plants and grasses, forms, as James Teit has written, a blanket over the planet.

February 12, 2011: Summit Hill, Victoria

Thick green leaves from bulbs poke through the grass at Summit Hill, but Fred Hook, an environmental technician with the City of Victoria, tells me they are English bluebells, not camas. He screws his face up with displeasure at the thought of the invasive bulb. Above us, the oak buds are still closed, but swelling. Their colour has changed in the last month from grey to light brown. One morning,

Burned meadow grasses at the Cowichan Garry Oak Preserve.

Meadow fires burn hot above the surface but not below the organic layer, thus preventing damage to plant roots and soil.

waking up early, I hear a song sparrow. Two mornings later, a winter wren calls for a half hour straight, despite the rain.

Invasive Species

Marauders, bullies, and aggressive invaders have changed the landscape of North America. Since their arrival these plants and animals have spread far beyond their original landing point; they are a bane to those who work in ecosystem restoration. We can take some solace in the countless organizations and individual gardeners who work in these landscapes and nurture camas bulbs from seed to first flower, with all the tenderness of a lover. Invasive flora and fauna, however, are just as eager to take over every square inch of land as they were when first transported here on Europe's ships.

The cost of invasive species management on the south coast is considerable. As of 2010, the Capital Regional District (CRD) had removed more than 50 tonnes of biomass from Mill Hill Regional Park, a prime Garry oak ecosystem. More than $260,000 has been provided in funding from Canada Habitat Stewardship program to support the effort. As of 2011, $57,000 has been spent in Beacon Hill Park alone for the removal of carpet burweed, a tenacious, prickly plant that grows in meadows and lodges in the skin of animals and humans alike. Thousands of volunteer hours have been logged in invasive species removal projects at sites around the region, including Trial Island, Beacon Hill Park, Uplands Park, Fort Rodd Hill, the Cowichan Garry Oak Preserve and the Mount Tzouhalem Ecological Reserve.

There are a number of invasive plants and animals that have done significant damage in Garry oak meadows; three — two plants and a mammal — stand out.

Scotch broom

Scotch broom demonstrates the extent to which invasive plants have affected south coast landscapes. This woody bush was introduced to North America by a homesick Scott, Captain Walter Grant, who was given a few seeds by the British Consul in the Sandwich Islands (Hawaii); he missed the low, brushy landscapes of his home and thought that broom might do well abroad. From the seeds given to him, three germinated, and over the course of the next century and a half, Scotch broom has spread across Vancouver Island, the Gulf Islands and the lower mainland to become the most significant flora threat to Garry oak ecosystems. Transported by truck wheels, mixed with dirt and gravel fill, carried by birds and animals, broom grows easily on disturbed soil sites and open fields. Its takeover was inadvertently aided by the provincial highways department, which used to plant broom as a bank stabilizer. Broom seed stays viable for up to 80 years; once established, it shades out native wildflowers and increases the nitrogen concentration in soils, eventually resulting in a mono-crop. Its seeds are toxic to livestock and horses; the plant is hardy and difficult to remove. To see its spread and effect, look to the hills above the Malahat, to clearcuts and disturbed soils on the Gulf Islands, to vacant lots and roadsides in our urban areas or in any regional park where restoration still is underway. Broom forms a potent and suffocating yellow carpet of flowers in May and June across the south islands. Many of the conservation scientists I talked to joked that the ultimate double-edged sword would be to find a commercial use for the stuff — it would help encourage removal but might also create a market for its cultivation.

House sparrows

House sparrows have been known to catch violet green swallows in mid air and plummet to the ground, where they peck the native birds to death. They also seek out native songbird nests, kill the young and peck open the eggs. Even when established in their own nest boxes, house sparrows still seek the deaths of other birds in an aggressive attempt to seize territory. We have all seen these sparrows on outdoor patios, at feeders, or in flocks in rattling bushes around the city, where they can produce a dozen or more new hatchlings each season, making them a tremendous threat to local songbird populations. When I catch them in the live box trap that my friend Malcolm lent me, I crush them between two logs and bury them in the raspberry patch. One house sparrow in North America is one house sparrow too many.

English ivy

English ivy, planted as a ground cover in gardens around the south coast, has encroached on many of our islands' most beautiful parks, sending a cascading, woven biomass across the forest and up into the trees. There, it latches into the cambium layers of the bark, growing more than 20 centimetres a month during summer, and essentially sucking the tree dry. Gorge waterway staff and volunteers have removed more than 14 tonnes of invasives, mostly consisting of ivy, from only 130 metres of shoreline at Point Ellis House, in an ongoing project. Once ivy reaches the second stage of its growth and goes to seed, it is virtually impossible to stop. Birds carry the seed far and wide, and the long tendrils thicken to an impenetrable mat.

*

All invasive plants and creatures once lived in the old world in relative stability, as the checks and balances of their original ecosystem prevented them from taking over. But once introduced to a new landscape, where those impediments are no longer present, they can do widespread damage to a delicately balanced ecosystem, blocking out light, discouraging competitors, altering the composition of soil and adding to landscape fragmentation.

It is no exaggeration to say that invasive species, next to development, have been the most overtly destructive force in Garry oak meadows. Certainly, their control and removal takes the lion's share of the money available for ecosystem restoration. Bolstering this removal effort are many programs that also focus on reintroduction and reestablishment of native species, which helps prevent invasives from regaining their hold. The most prominent and ambitious of these is the Victoria-based Garry Oak Ecosystems Recovery Team (GOERT), a largely federally funded organization that uses an ecosystem-based approach to protect species at risk across the south island and Gulf Islands.

Parks staff removing invasive Scotch broom from Mill Hill Regional Park, 2011.

GOERT was formed in the same time period as the Species at Risk Act (SARA) was being created in Canada (BC is one of only two Canadian provinces without stand-alone endangered species legislation). According to Marilyn Fuchs, a founding member of GOERT and biologist with Capital Regional District Parks, the federal act's philosophy fits perfectly with Garry oak ecosystems, and the number of listed species in the meadows made the ecosystem a good candidate for funding. Thus was GOERT able to emerge in tandem with the Species at Risk Act, forging connec-

When Garry oak meadows are disturbed or removed during development, invasive species take hold. Scotch broom colonizing the Salt Spring Island Channel Ridge development site.

tions with relevant government departments.

Two models provided the framework for GOERT: the South Okanogan Similkameen Conservation Program and the Tall Grass Prairie Program in Ontario. The result was both a fine- and coarse-filter strategy — to protect whole ecosystems through invasives removal and large-scale restoration but also to focus on the species at risk within the plant community. Despite the work of GOERT, Garry oak ecosystems, in terms of western knowledge, are still not comprehensively understood or managed. One of Fuch's laments is that there often isn't time or resources for plant-community classification work, which could determine which plants would and ought to be growing in a particular area. Some preserves, like Cowichan and Tzouhalem, are understood extremely well by their caretakers, which allows restoration that uses plant-community classification knowledge. More often, restoration involves only the crude work of removing invasives and monitoring existing listed species. Government funding limitations determine which species get attention; maintenance of species numbers is supported, rather than expansion of plant communities, even if the species are red-listed.

Fuchs has hope, though it is small, for the future of this and other ecosystems. "We are on a crash course toward destruction," she says one day in her Esquimalt back garden, with its dark green canopy of oaks that extends into Cairn Park. She wants to see a complete cultural shift in how we organize our affairs, a turn away from the growth and consumption model western society has taken so to heart. But it is not as simple, she admits, as an outright ban on further development in the remaining meadows. The intricate connection between ecosystems needs a more comprehensive solution.

Nomenclature & History

Mill Hill, in Colwood, is one of the primary regional parks on the south island where extensive Garry oak rocky outcrop ecosystem restoration is taking place. In February's north wind and sun, I walk the 200-metre rise of the summit trail to the open peak — a small island of natural beauty sandwiched between Colwood and Langford's sprawl. Common camas, Camassia quamash, *are coming up everywhere; their leaves already four inches high. There are the beginnings of sea blush, satin flower, shooting star and fawn lilies. All leaf, no bud. Broom however, is also everywhere. Semi-leafless in the early spring, it casts a thin shadow over the moss and carpet of oak leaves like green, waving, fan coral. In some hollows by the edge of the trail, there are piles of cut broom, left from the last volunteer "broom pull," which occurs now twice a year, and usually attracts dozens of people willing to spend their weekend lopping off the bush at the root level and piling it for disposal by helicopter. I can see the areas that have been cleared, but the extent of the remaining coverage is daunting.*

The oaks are still closed-bud up here, their trunks smaller and more gnarled than those in more protected meadows. The view from the top is almost 360 degrees — Esquimalt Harbour, Victoria, Mount Work, Sugarloaf Mountain, Metchosin. Despite the wind, the sun feels like spring.

Since the first days of agriculture, when receding ice across the continents led to the Neolithic period and to the cultivation of squashes and corn in Mexico, which began around 7,000 BCE, humans have been searching for ways to learn about and name plants. Our need stemmed from hunger but also from human desire for beauty and our need to heal. To know one flower from another could mean the difference between life and death, as with the death camas and common camas. To understand a plant in its place in the world, we must understand that for millennia we have sought to cure illness with flowers and roots, to breed ornamental lilies for their longest and brightest blooms and to identify and cultivate the bushes and trees that would bear the best fruit.

Aristotle also asserts, at the beginning of his *Metaphysics*, that "all men by nature desire to know." To learn of plants is more than simply fulfilling basic needs and aesthetic preference; it is a desire to find relation. What is one plant's relationship to another? How can they be grouped? Where do they grow? How do we differentiate between them?

Our earliest written collection of knowledge on the plant world

Satin flower (Sisyrinchium douglasii) in Devonian Regional Park.

Beacon Hill Park oaks, winter.
PHOTO BY EMRYS MILLER

came from Theophrastus, a scholar working in the Peripatetic School at the Lyceum in 347 BCE, alongside Aristotle and in the wake of Plato's texts. Theophrastus gave the western world its first serious written descriptions of plants, their preferred habitat, and their uses. It was he who first suggested that all wild plants, most of which were at the time unnamed, should be worthy of the same close attention given to cultivated varieties. Everything deserved a name and a description. From him we have the words *iris, narkissos, elleboros* and *anemone*.

When it comes to the natural world, our thinking did not always rely upon the rigorous scientific method that takes prominence today. Hesiod thought that oaks produced not only acorns but also honey and bees. Andrea Cesalpino (1519-1603) believed that seeds from many trees were directly extruded from the pith through the softer bark of small branches. As late as the 1800s, it was believed that swallows, a key avian species in Garry oak meadows, did not migrate south but rather wintered underwater, at the bottom of ponds and rivers. Flying low over vernal pools and rivers, swallows will dip and scoop insects off the surface; at dusk, they seem to disappear against the inky depths. It must have been tempting to believe that they, too, had found a way of enduring the cold, northern European winters; that they did not leave us, but transformed themselves and sank to their small safety of reeds until spring.

Our western knowledge of Garry oak ecosystems has been, in some ways, no more complete. Hans Roemer's study of Saanich Peninsula forests was published in 1974, but it was the first such study of Garry oak meadows as a whole. There are hundreds of Garry oak ecosystems across the south island that have not been completely mapped. Indeed, the one common grievance I heard expressed by botanists, ecologists and geographers was a lack of comprehensive knowledge about the ecosystem. Much time and money is spent on tracking and caring for specific listed species. We need, researchers told me, more broad knowledge. We need to know more about *relation*.

For over a millennium after the death of Theophrastus, there were only brief flashes of serious interest in a factual classifying and ordering of the world of plants; too much relied primarily upon myth, legend, superstition and mistaken copies of texts from the past. What survived of Theophrastus' work was finally published again in Latin in 1483 in Treviso, Italy, by Cesalpino. He created the first attempt at a two-part naming system, which brought us names such as *Sisyrinchium californicum* (golden-eyed grass) and *Sisyrinchium douglasii*, (satin flower or Douglas's blue-eyed grass). These are two species of lily from the same family: one found in wetland and marshes, the other a common spring flower in Garry oak meadows.

Carl Linnaeus (1707-1778) refined this structure into the basis of our modern species classification system. His *Species Plantarum*, published in 1737, gave us kingdom, phylum, class, order, family, genus, species — divisions we all remember from high school biology class. With the advent of genetic testing, the species in these divisions are being further adjusted and regrouped.

But the journey does not end here. The scientific classification system provides us with an intricate map of every individual species we have the means to categorize. It does not, however, explore the connections between these species or their relationship to the larger ecosystem.

Alexander Humboldt

One of the primary issues facing restoration projects in Garry
oak ecosystems today stems from the philosophical divide between
species and ecosystem schools of thought; the problem has been
debated for generations. One regards individual species as the
most important element in an ecosystem; the other continues the
work of those such as Alexander Humboldt (1769–1859). Taking as
his inspiration German Romantic philosophy of the time, including poet Rilke and philosopher Hegel, Humboldt introduced continental Europe to the idea of plant study — botany — as a holistic
science. Humboldt argued that plant communities needed to be
viewed as a cohesive system larger than the sum of their parts.
Humboldt's Formation tradition was closely connected with the
Romantic reaction to the Enlightenment. Called Organicism by
its followers, Formation theory emphasizes connections between
ecosystems and regions; the discovery of a rare species such as
Howell's triteleia (*Triteleia howellii*) is less important than discov-
ering the relationships between environmental factors and geography. *Why* a species grows where it does becomes as important as
the flower itself. From Humboldt, we have the famous axiom of
many present-day ecological movements: "Everything is related."

Humboldt did not use the term ecosystem — this word was
not coined until nearly 150 years later, when it was embraced in
the 1960s as a viable area of research in biology. It grew in stature
through the 1980s and is now recognized as essential in botany's
vocabulary. By giving credence to the idea of Organicism, and to
the term ecosystem, we are closer to looking at landscapes holisti-
cally — a forest, or an oak meadow, is more than just the tree and
flower species that occur within its boundaries, it is a cooperative
unit, a working whole.

The understanding of an interdependent ecosystem — with biodiversity and ecological integrity central to its health — is shared
by a host of contemporary environmental scientists and writers.
John Muir writes, "When one tugs at a single thing in nature, he
finds it attached to the rest of the world." Studying individual species has a strong draw, and the strange sexiness of watching their
numbers climb due to restoration efforts is undeniable, but we
need broad, ecosystem-based knowledge in order to do justice to a

system that has proved much more complex than Sir James Douglas could ever have imagined.

Beacon Hill Park oaks, spring.

Hans Roemer, author of *Forest Vegetation and Environments of the Saanich Peninsula, Vancouver Island,* found a similar divide between the species and formation schools in Europe and North America and sought to amend it with his own research. In North America, with its vast geography, inaccessibility, and new flora, plant characteristics were studied far more often than the relationships between a plant and its community. Thus, before Roemer's study, we knew the species that were likely to occur in a meadow, but we did not necessarily have the description and classification of the ecosystem itself. Roemer attempted to fill this gap. His work is the first examination on the Saanich Peninsula of the "dynamic relationships between existing communities."

Roemer found that properly correlating plant species with habitat features depended on everything: climate, geology, soil, ground water levels, marine deposits, light conditions and human interaction. Plant cover in turn affected the micro-climate on the forest floor, with open Garry oak stands creating a climate that had more in common with a meadow than a forest.

However, Roemer's 1972 study couldn't fully address some questions. The term Traditional Ecological Knowledge (TEK) — knowledge of a land by Aboriginal peoples whose history involved close contact with local ecosystems — was not yet in common use. Roemer could only suppose why, when Sir James Douglas landed in Victoria, large swaths of open oak parkland existed where, based on both soil and climate conditions, Douglas fir should have predominated. Was it grazing from large game populations? Summer drought? Camas harvesting? Roemer labeled the mature, open oak landscape that Europeans found as an "anthropo- and zoobiotic climax", which essentially means that it got that way through influence by animals and humans "in a culture which was still in full harmony with the natural environment." His study ends here, opening the door for a new way of seeing a supposedly unmanaged landscape. The full history of First Nations' interdependent relationship with their land is only now beginning to come to light.

Gardens Past

The dreams clash
          and are shattered —
and that I tried to make a paradiso
                              terrestre.
                    (POUND, *Cantos* 802)

FEBRUARY 26, 2011, MOUNT DOUG, SAANICH

An unexpected snowfall on the 23rd has left the whole region blan-
keted in white. Usually, with a late snow like this, the flakes fall
heavy and the temperature warms almost immediately, after the city
plummets briefly into chaos. This year, the mercury dips to minus 15
with wind chill and the streets turn to ice. New leaves on the Indian
plum bushes in the lower meadows freeze and turn a watery green.
The snow spins as powder under fierce wind, and a layer of ice coats
the forest floor. Everything that I've been watching come up the last
three weeks seems to suffer under this late-season blast of arctic air.

  I climb the upper slopes of Mount Douglas Park, where fir gives
way to snow and an unprotected upper rocky meadow of oak and
broom. No greenery is visible and a northeast wind howls. Some-
one's dog races past. Things feel eerily stalled; a slice of Haro Strait
lies like an aquamarine ribbon below the cloud and fog. Never
have the meadows felt so inhospitable, so unlikely to support such a
diverse array of life.

Much in history has determined our current relationship with Garry oak meadows. European descendants in North America, being from elsewhere, have a history of dislocation. Our ancestors left the old world seeking something better — a new paradise. On Vancouver Island, for instance, we cut down swaths of forest, creating stump-ridden clearings, then dynamited the trunks to make room for crops and grazing fields. We climbed the remaining oak trunks and hunted deer. We created roads, railways and villages, planted wheat and corn and around our houses, scattered imported seeds and planted cultivated fruit and flower bushes in our gardens. But why remake a world that had already been recognized, by Sir James Douglas and many others, as so beautiful?

1. Homesickness

Many of our ancestors took seeds from the old world in an attempt to recreate what we were most homesick for: the old country. Garry oak meadows were seen, then forgotten — as if we had been blinded — in favour of something remembered. It is the act of one who tries to remake a new lover in the image of one lost. Had we looked hard, as a few of the time did, we might have seen that the new world had as much to offer as the old. Our homesickness was both need for the familiar, and a less gentle need to colonize and remake something in our own image, to foster the spread of old-world plants, religion and culture. English Hawthorne, St. John's Wort and Periwinkle all began in the new world as seeds carried from the old. Surrounding oneself with familiar plants, and shaping the landscape into a simulacrum of a recognizable Eden, helped assuage homesickness. It also prevented a full appreciation of the flora that lay outside each cultivated garden.

2. Perfection and Mortality

Endless productivity leads to endless consumption, which leaves space for neither death nor imperfection. We have found ourselves on a quest for a kind of immortality through the production of constantly new, unblemished beauty — Robert Pogue Harrison, in *Gardens,* gives the example of flower beds in cities that use perpetually in-bloom plants to create an artificial garden, where neither death nor decay are ever featured or seen. By perpetuating this standard, we remove ourselves from the natural cycles that a true garden would give us, natural cycles in which we might participate. There is no space in this way of thinking for the Japanese concept of *wabi sabi* — the slightly melancholy beauty that inhabits something imperfect and transient. There is no gardener in our unblemished flowerbeds, tending and coaxing. The scene is grown by formula, planted at height of colour and removed when it no longer presents our recreated paradise.

When it comes to our oaks and their habitat, this need for perfection becomes apparent in the way both are viewed by many residents around the south island. The trees are messy, cragged, crooked; their acorns and small branches and leaves are raked and carted away from the very roots that need them. So, too, the deeper meadows, which are, in almost all neighbourhoods, mowed into submission, covered with bark mulch or landscaped into English country garden glory. We have, as a culture, very little time or patience for living amidst the processes of this region's natural landscapes. We would rather fill it with our own version of paradise, which requires the undoing, consuming and remaking of this island's original garden — the oak tree glade — in our own perpetually dissatisfied image.

3. *Care*

Care, writes Harrison, is the solution to this unending cycle, for one cannot consume what one is trying to care for. Care also demands a kind of activity that surpasses the lethargic vision of original Eden. One must be involved in order to maintain, coax, nurture and nourish a garden. One must take an active part. Harrison is not the first person to cite *care* as a keystone concept in our relations with the world. The American poet Alan Grossman calls care the fundamental principle by which poetry may successfully unfold. Art that works within the morality of care demands a kind of openness to the world. It is a whole-hearted engagement with that which it cares for. It is, by necessity, devoid of ego, empty of the moral value of work, free from virtue. The worker, as Harrison writes, is "altogether handed over to his garden." He is "committed to the welfare of what he nourishes to life."

The giant, Cowichan Garry Oak Preserve, Duncan.

As in art, so with the world. To interact with Garry oak meadows with the self-possession and sense of responsibility that care demands is to participate fully our world. As in Italo Calvino's *Invisible Cities*, we must seek out those things which are *not* the "inferno" of unending destruction, aimlessness and consumption, "then make them endure, give them space."

MARCH 5, 2011, COWICHAN GARRY OAK PRESERVE, DUNCAN

I'm standing with the Nature Conservancy of Canada's Tim Ennis and the Cowichan Nation's Clayton George at the edge of an old hayfield in the Cowichan Valley, about halfway between Mount Tzouhalem and Mount Tuam. Below us, the field stretches in unbroken waves of snow-flattened grass, a thick pelt that runs right to the edge of Quamichan Lake. The rain has briefly stopped. Low scudding clouds draw shadow patches over the gold and tired green expanse.

At regular intervals, like monoliths in the otherwise bare field, stand perhaps half a dozen oaks, their enormous trunks easily eight feet in diameter. Their branches carve high into the air and seem to inhabit the entire vertical space between ground and cloud. In the centre of the field stands one giant, purportedly the largest Garry oak in the world. Some estimates place its age at 800 years, which means it was alive before the advent of the printing press and the industrial revolution, before Columbus, before the Renaissance. All of the trees in this field have enormous burls — rounded, blackened distensions of the bark and trunk. Ennis tells me that these burls, often found in older trees, may be a result of years of controlled burns in the camas fields. The trees develop a scar of sorts, both as reaction to and protection against regular, low intensity fires that cleared the meadows of smaller brush.

We walk to the giant across muddy fields past a number of experimental plots and various types of cages. They are, says Tim, trying to figure out what eats small oak seedlings. Is it rabbit, deer, raccoon? He guesses rabbit, who strip the bark from seedlings, effectively girding them before they can grow large enough to withstand predators, but there are fences specific to each species. A small seep extends across the field, drifting a diagonal glaze of water on its journey to the lake. We step across and walk to the base of the tree. Clayton George has never been here before, but for Tim, it's old hat. An award winning photo by one of the conservancy's staff was taken of him during an experimental controlled burn last summer, smoke drifting through the tree's branches and the blue sky heightened in colour by orange flames.

Up close, it's hard to know what to do. I would like to climb up and fall asleep in one of the giant crotches. I would like it to be warm, and dry, so I could lie below it in the grass. Instead, I take photos. Circling to the other side of the trunk, he shows us a series of rebar footholds driven deep into the trunk. For climbing, so that hunters could sit up high and sight deer. The ground is littered with branches from the winter's storms, fallen from the oak's upper canopy. Many are as thick as the trunks of the oaks I've seen down in Victoria. The rain moves in again and we turn back. A week later, I realize that in my rush to ask questions and take photos, I forgot to touch, even once, its pitted, whorled constellation of a trunk.

Eden Lost

Right now, we value earlier peoples for a lot of things — for
their values and their culture, for their bravery and resource-
fulness in war, for their spiritual connection to nature, for
their dances and ceremonies, for the dramatic and colour-
ful nature of their adornment. But when it comes to how
they managed the environment, the thing most of us value
about those peoples is the perception that there were so few
of them they couldn't really mess things up. In other words,
we value them for being a failure, because that's what most
of us assume they were. [But] earlier Gardeners didn't just
impact the environment, they shaped it. In some instances
they created it. By so doing, they weren't a failure. They were
a success — in some cases an unsurpassed success. Those
successes deserve to be studied, not as primitive curiosities,
but as examples of effective management worthy of understanding and emulation.

— DAN DAGGET, *Gardeners of Eden*

Recent research on the history of human civilization in North
America during the last 10,000 years argues that the primary inhabitants of this continent shared many of Harrison's and Grossman's
principles of care, treating the world around them as a garden
that could be tended for the benefit of all. According to anthropological botanist Charles R. Clement, cave inhabitants from 4,000
years ago realized that they could get much more productivity out
of the poor soil of the South American forests by growing fruit,
nut and palm trees than they could using traditional agriculture.
The result of their efforts is what we now call the "wild" Amazon
rain forest. Soil geographer William I. Woods has also argued that
the indigenous people of the Amazon rainforest were also respon-
sible for creating *terra preta*, a rich, fertile "black earth" that, "at
some threshold level . . . attains the capacity to perpetuate — even
regenerate itself — thus behaving more like a living 'super'-organ-
ism than an inert material." This soil was not only created but was
deposited into areas of poor soil — the way a sourdough starter
can inoculate a new batch of dough — in order to improve yields.

Examples of this interrelatedness span the globe; humans are a "keystone species," according to wildlife ecologist Charles Kay, that have a far reaching effect on the survival and number of many other species. Our role as a keystone species is exemplified on this continent by our effect upon buffalo, passenger pigeons and elk. Populations of these species soared after the first wave of disease depleted aboriginal populations, which had previously kept their numbers in check. As journalist Charles Mann writes, when human influence and ability to care is removed — as it was after the disease epidemics of smallpox, measles and flu that reached both ends of the continent — the results are severe and lasting.

When Europeans moved west, they were preceded by two waves: one of disease, the other of ecological disturbance. The former crested with fearsome rapidity; the latter sometimes took more than a century to quiet down. Far from destroying pristine wilderness, European settlers bloodily created it. By 1800 the hemisphere was chockablock with new wilderness. If "forest primeval" means a woodland unsullied by the human presence, William Denevan has written, there

Camas emerging from a winter carpet of fallen Garry oak leaves.

was much more of it in the late eighteenth century than in the early sixteenth.
— CHARLES MANN, *1491: New Revelations of the Americas Before Columbus*

The Garry oak meadow is just one example of a managed landscape that Europeans mistook for a "wild" ecosystem. Nancy Turner argues that the problem may have partly been one of limited imagination:

> Seen through European eyes, neither the Aboriginal peoples' use of the land, nor their ownership of it, was considered valid or legitimate, perhaps because it was so different from their own. In most cases, the newcomers recognized only large, permanent settlements and highly visible agricultural modification as criteria for land ownership. This demonstrates the important connections between land ownership and the question of cultivation and land management.
> — NANCY TURNER, "Traditional Ecological Knowledge and Wisdom of Aboriginal Peoples in British Columbia"

First Nations worked with the land rather than against it, nurturing their own version of a garden and creating a cultivated, managed space. Deep-soil Garry oak meadows are one of the primary culturally modified landscapes of the south coast. Though they may have appeared as wild and unsettled, meadows were maintained as open parkland through concerted ongoing efforts. Passed from generation to generation through the matrilineal Coast Salish, their boundaries were carefully marked and each plot intensively tended for cultivation of food and medicinal crops. These enclosures were attended to by both the living — for food production — and the dead, through the burial cairns that dot their expanses. In short, human beings played a keystone species role in the cultivation of the look and feel of the meadows, as well as the prevalent species that thrived within them.

Meadows were kept clear by the Coast Salish for thousands of years before the arrival of Europeans, and served as a food source for many First Nations up and down the west coast and into the Interior. Again, Turner writes that camas bulbs were "especially

Camas was harvested and used in many areas of BC, Washington, Oregon, California, Idaho and Montana. Here, Annie Yellow Bear pounds camas bulbs, Kamiah, Idaho, ca. 1890. NATIONAL PARK SERVICE (US), NEZ PERCE NATIONAL HISTORICAL PARK; PHOTO NO. NEPE-HI-0773

important to the Coast Salish of southern Vancouver Island, but were eaten to a lesser extent by the mainland Halq-emyelem, Squamish, Sechelt, Comox, Nuu-chah-nulth and Kwakwaka'wakw," as well as the Interior Kootenai and Salish of Washington and Montana. In the Cowichan's case, the ecologists Pojar and MacKinnon estimate that 15,000 people originally lived in the meadows' midst and depended on the summer harvest of camas. As with the Amazon rainforest, fields had to be managed and cultivated in order to support such large populations. "Harvesting the bulbs was a seasonal event often involving setting up temporary living shelters," and "could last for several weeks, with entire families participating." Each year, communities would dig and harvest larger bulbs during or soon after flowering, in order to differentiate them from death camas, a poisonous, white flowering variety. Sod was removed and bulbs dug using oak-wood sticks. Smaller bulbs were replanted for future harvests. Splitting the bulbs aided their health in the same way that splitting tulips encourages greater flowering. The act of disturbing the ground may also have played a part in the success of camas growth, as removing stones during digging and cultivation loosened the soil.

Harvested bulbs were steamed in large pits, which were lined with seaweed, blackberry, salal berry branches and ferns; bulbs were piled on the top, in amounts up to 50 kilograms. The pit was then covered with branches, soil or mats and a fire lit over the top. Once the pit was hot, water was poured in and the bulbs steamed for a day and a half before being eaten. Dried bulbs were also traded, along with salmon and other foods, up and down the coast. In the Willamette Valley of Oregon, camas steaming pits, as well as charred remains of the bulbs, date back 7,750 years. The bulbs contain the complex sugar inulin, which must be heated to become digestible; once cooked, they taste somewhat like a baked pear or a sweet potato.

Similar food production and cultivation of land occurred up and down the BC coast, as Kwakwaka'wakw historian Daisy Sewid-Smith noted in conversation with Nancy Turner, but as with Garry oak meadow management, Europeans found First Nations' techniques hard to comprehend. "But, see, people — this is what I'm saying — people didn't believe that we did this. They think that Nature just grows on its own. But our people felt to get more harvest, and bigger berries, they did these things. Same thing a farmer does." Despite the historically interconnected relationship between the meadows and the people that managed them, modern day environmental thinking has primarily focused on removing human influence from protected land. The accepted solution for overpopulation troubles, for species collapse and ecosystem disappearance has been to set pieces of land aside, remove the invasive species and leave it alone. First Nations management of Garry oak meadows, however, is an excellent example of holistic engagement with the natural world, one that actually *requires* human participation. Historically, a meadow was cared for so that it might flourish and feed the families who depended on its health for their survival. Societies were committed to its welfare; similarly, its open form depended on their need. In the case of deep-soil meadows, the need for food created the landscape in which it grew. Human involvement in this ecosystem's development is a fact that calls into question many of the environmental management policies currently in place in Garry oak ecological reserves and other protected areas.

Is it our regret for past damages that leads us to minimize our relationship to nature? Do we feel so much guilt over our trespasses that we think it better to try to erase our mark on those small patches that have been set aside? Many parks in BC feature limited human access; some areas of the Sea to Sea Wilderness, on Vancouver Island's Sooke Hills, are closed to the public; we have grizzly reserves and caribou preserves where humans are told to leave no trace or to stay away all together. But the flip side of this argument is that by staying away, we also erase ourselves from the list of natural species on this earth. We make ourselves the other, an interloper. Thus are we in danger of abandoning our place in the natural world and our responsibilities to the planet, responsibilities, as Dan Dagget argues, "we evolved to uphold." Countless volunteers, organizations and scientists are all proving that we can have a tremendously beneficial effect on Garry oak ecosystems when we work to remove the invasive species and restore original flora and fauna populations. But we need to question, in this modern age, our true reasons for participating in this restoration effort. Though camas may, we hope, continue to be eaten as a traditional food among First Nations, we have no need to depend, nor could we, on its harvest in order to provide our carbohydrate needs. Many of the other species that used to provide sustenance, such as riceroot (chocolate lily) and deltoid balsamroot, are no longer plentiful enough to sustain significant harvest. They may never be again. But if not for food, what do we keep in our minds as the reasons to restore these species?

Restoration

Sweetness. As I shimmy under the barbed-wire fence that rings the edge of the old upper battery station and skid down the ledge into a bowl of untamed winter grass that separates oak glade from cultivated hilltop, the scent hits me like a wall. Moist earth, miner's lettuce, sunlit camas leaves half a foot high. What is it that brings the sweet smell? There is nothing in bloom, but the earth itself seems to be steaming despite the cool wind. Jumping from ancient rock wall to brick pile to moss cushion to forest floor, I hear a pileated woodpecker, chickadees singing their spring mating song, juncos. The warmth rises and coats the air, as if setting the world aflame.

There are many examples on the southwest coast where Garry oak meadows have been lost, mostly due to a tide of increasingly aggressive development. On Channel Ridge, Salt Spring Island, a moonscape of quarried rock and invasive species greets hikers. On Bear Mountain, public uproar followed the dynamiting of a Karst cave, sacred to First Nations, and its surrounding Garry oak upland meadows. The cave and meadows were part of the Bear Mountain Resort development, bankrolled by former Tampa Bay Lightning owner and professional hockey player Len Barrie. Along with the Bear Mountain interchange, the developments spurred accusations of "inadequate public input, due process and democratic principles," according to the *Victoria Times-Colonist*. In 2012, the development company went bankrupt and Barrie lost his house on the mountain, but the development remains. Further examples of losses within the last decade include developments on Christmas Hill, Mount Helmcken, Little Skirt Mountain, and the land on which the Millstream Road commercial district now stands.

Oaks have a hard time even in their namesake municipality. Oak Bay, a sleepy set of neighbourhoods east of downtown Victoria, recently endured the attempts of consultant Michael Prescott to repopulate the neighbourhood with palm trees. Citing global warming, Prescott argued that palms were the best tree to line Oak Bay Avenue from its start all the way to its finish near Cattle Point. To help his fellow citizens in the charge, he began selling palm seedlings on the front lawn of the municipal hall, with proceeds going to the Fifth Oak Bay Scout Troop and the Oak Bay Rotary Club. The significance of the names, apparently, was lost on him. Oak Bay councillors agreed to the sale on the condition that Garry oak seedlings were given away alongside the palms. The man to give the oaks away was District of Saanich arborist Ron Carter. The two worked amicably together for a couple of spring sales, until the cold snap of November 2008, when most of the palm tree seedlings that Prescott had sold died. The following spring, no palms were for sale.

Science and Ethics

Ecosystems share many of the features and puzzles presented by an immune system or a central nervous system. They exhibit the same overwhelming diversity. We have yet to assay the range of organisms present in a cubic meter of temperate-zone soil, let alone the incredible arrays of species in a tropical forest. Ecosystems are continually in flux and exhibit a wondrous panoply of interactions such as mutualism, parasitism, biological arms races, and mimicry. Matter, energy, and information are shunted around in complex cycles. Once again, the whole is more than the sum of its parts.

– JOHN HOLLAND, *Hidden Order: How Adaptation Builds Complexity*

Volunteers hauling away invasive English ivy, Trial Island.

Speak to scientists working in oak ecosystems, or indeed in any ecosystem under threat around the world, and a common argument for protection tends to surface: our primary work must be to protect and stabilize any species that is rare or under threat. Our debt to other creatures on this planet is large, and many argue we have an obligation, as reasoning beings, to protect and nurture the natural world. Its survival, and many say our own, depends on sustaining biodiversity. For some, however, this concentration on only the rare inhabitants in an ecosystem is frustrating. Vancouver and Victoria ecologists Terry McIntosh and Adolf Ceska both argue that more funding and time needs to be given to the study of an ecosystem as a whole. "You could remove all the listed species from an ecosystem," McIntosh told me, "and that ecosystem would still function just fine. No one species is any more important than another. And protecting a rare species doesn't necessarily mean that the whole ecosystem is being protected." For others, such as botanist Matt Fairbarns, who works extensively on Trial Island, rare species, their protection and their reintroduction into habitats, is an integral part of restoration efforts. *In situ*, Fairbarns's view is persuasive.

Trial Island Ecological Reserve

The clouds hang in a thick line along the entire southern shore of Vancouver Island, but out on the water in a speeding zodiac, we are bathed in sun. "This is the secret of Trial Island," says Fairbarns, volunteer ecosystem restoration manager of the Trial Island Ecological Reserve. "It's often sunny here when it's pouring just across the passage. It's why we call it the Salish Riviera." A thirty-knot wind is kicking up from the southwest, and by the time we reach the beach on the west side, the swells push the boat well onto the cobbles, where we unload knapsacks, secateurs, work gloves and twenty people, all of whom have given over eight hours of their Saturday to the task of ripping English ivy from the soil of a small ravine, vine by painstaking vine. Many of the volunteers are back here for the fourth or fifth time. "It's a great feeling to go back to the same place year after year, and see the recovery of an area I've worked on," Ian Cruickshank told me. And this recovery, which Fairbarns shows us on a walk during our lunch break, is compelling.

Trial Island lies just off the south coast of Oak Bay. It is owned by both the federal and provincial governments; a communications company leases part of the provincial land for broadcast towers, which soar a couple of hundred feet into the air, their guy wires studded into the ground. From Trial's near shores, one looks across the narrow passage — which during flood and ebb tide turns into a fleet-flowing river — to the manicured lawns of the Oak Bay golf course, its surrounding neighbourhoods and the rocky cliffs of Anderson Hill. It is both very near to and very far from the city and its consequences, and this has made it a mecca when it comes to species diversity. Trial Island, along with Valpol Island in southwestern Ontario, has the highest concentration of rare species in Canada. The ecological reserve was established on the island's south end in 1990 to protect these species. The southernmost tip features a federal light station; the keeper joins us for much of the day. Twenty blue- and red-listed species of plants make their home here, including white-top aster, paintbrush owl-clover, golden paintbrush, creeping wild rye, rosy owl clover, California buttercup, bear's-foot sanicle, purple sanicle, and Scouler's campion. Nine distinct plant communities make their home here, but the Garry oak ecosystem is the most extensive.

Trial has two vernal pool systems, open, deep-soil meadows, rocky bluffs, dwarf Garry oaks, and wind. It is the wind that has shaped the island's ecosystems perhaps most extensively. It pours over the lowland 23 hectares and ripples the camas leaves in gleaming, flattened waves. Wind has kept the oaks from growing higher than eight feet, and everything that has height also has an easterly lean, pushed over the years into strange, twisted shapes by the constant pressure. Trial is like nothing I've seen before. It feels untouched, despite the proximity of the city, the mown path from light station to bay, and the hundreds of invasive Canadian geese that sit placidly in its meadows, eating some of those listed species down to nubs in the soil. The meadows continue to the water's edge, where the rocky shore lowers into blue water; swells on the west side often reach eight feet in height, and when the wind gusts it is hard to stay upright.

I find myself mesmerized by the incredible variety of rare plants found on Trial. It is like being at an outdoor herbarium, on a treasure hunt of sorts. We tiptoe along the trails and hop from bare rock to rock when Fairbarns leads us to a patch of something rare. The reaction to each discovery is small — these are scientists — but intense. Many people thrust cameras down, to snap a picture of a tiny leaf or flower. I join the fray.

Golden paintbrush (*Castilleja levisecta*), akin to common red paintbrush, makes its home on Trial Island and one other location in Canada. At last count there were five thousand plants on Trial. Rosy owl clover (*Orthocarpus bracteosus*), a slender, purple, annual herb, occurs only here, in all of Canada. Seaside birds-foot lotus occurs in only five locations across the country; one is here. The list goes on: white top aster, which can take up to 50 years to reproduce; black knotweed, seaside birds-foot trefoil, a single green sprout that Fairbarns points out on our walk, bear's-foot sanicle, which occurs in patches, along with the dense-flowered lupine in the field on which the coastguard helicopter lands. "In spring I try to get them to land somewhere else," the keeper tells us. The lupine is a bundle of grey, silvery leaf clusters, sitting on top of a lily-pad-like base. It is perhaps an inch or so high, but will grow to a couple of feet, with yellowy, pinkish flowers. Once she points them out, I begin to see them all over the field. Yellow flags

have been placed at the edge of the path, to prevent them from being walked on by lighthouse or communications tower staff. Bear's-foot sanicle, or footprint of spring (*Sanicula arctopoides*), has the same egg-yolk-yellow of the more common spring gold, but a low, spreading habit, surrounded by toothed, yellowy-green leaves. Not exactly an annual, but not a perennial, it lives for a decade or more before finally flowering, setting seed and dying all in one season. The geese, says Fairbarns, often eat the flowering heads. Along with the ivy-pulling volunteers, there is also a woman here to count the sanicle. By the end of the day, she has covered the southern half of the island; the count is more than four hundred.

Trial Island volunteers on a nature walk, led by Matt Fairbarns.

Restoration of the ecological reserve began in earnest in 2003, when volunteers began by removing Scotch broom. On our walk, Fairbarns shows us areas that were infested just three years ago. There is no sign of disturbance now — camas ripples above the rolling fields, the green so green it's almost blue. I spot the first open flowers, along with shooting stars, fawn lilies, spring gold and chocolate lilies. Most of the endangered species that Fairbarns shows us, however, are bundles of leaves just emerging from the ground, or in some cases, a single, tiny leaflet. We must use our imaginations to visualize the full bloom. The volunteers range in age from early-20s biology students to late-60s retirees. There are staff from GOERT and BC Parks, and many who have also taken Fairbarns' past summer employment offers, when he brings teams back to Trial for a week to two weeks of sustained invasive species removal and restoration.

Bear's foot sanicle (Sanicula arctopoides) in the helicopter landing field, Trial Island.

We work in two hollows on the lee side of the island, next to the shoreline, where the land falls down from its 20-foot height to small ravines. The ivy is matted and intertwined three feet deep. To remove the plant, one grabs a vine and simply pulls, rather than cuts. The record by the end of the day is a 25-foot twisted, ropy stem. We pile the removed biomass in giant, woven bags; when they fill, we haul them up the ravine to a pile, much of which looks to be several years old. "It's hard to get BC Parks interested in burning the removed biomass, even though that's what we're supposed to do," Fairbarns tells me. "They don't like to burn in spring, for danger of fire, and they don't like to burn in fall,

because it's too hard to get here in winter storms." So the pile, perhaps 20 feet square, grows larger and taller. Once the bulk of the ivy is removed from a patch of ground, the remaining stalks are cut to the earth, leaving bare soil with the occasional native bulb leaf and Nootka Rose standing like sentinels. Fairbarns will return in fall to paint the re-sprouting ivy with a herbicide, killing only the plant and not whatever native species have survived cover. The ivy presents a more challenging situation than the broom in many ways. It forms a thicker mat that prevents sunlight from reaching the ground. It tends to infiltrate the soil more, like a cancer, and thus leaves less room for native bulbs. Once it's gone, some species will move back in naturally — camas being one of them; others will have to be reintroduced through plantings.

By the end of the day, we have cleared two areas of about 400 square feet. Around us, amidst snowberry, rose, alder and oak, the thatch of ivy reaches under the branches of the trees and over the tops of their canopies, obscuring everything but the vague shapes of the plants below. I ask Cruickshank, an endearingly enthusiastic volunteer, why he's here. "I'm taking college prerequisites for science programs right now." He stops pulling and smiles. "I don't really know what I want to do — environmental studies, ecology — it doesn't matter, as long as I can do a job that lets me be outside, taking care of native species and restoring ecosystems." Fairbarns looks up smiling: "That'll work as long as you're fine with being paid a volunteer's wages."

Here is one drawback of ecosystem restoration that is species-based. The goal of the federal program, Fairbarns tells me, is to maintain populations of listed species in a given reserve, not to improve the numbers. Thus, if a site has already suffered from plummeting numbers, a federally funded program will do little to restore previous population levels. As well, there is little funding to measure existing populations or success in restoration efforts. The lack of follow through, Fairbarns says, may cause trouble for restoration organizations that are primarily government-funded, as independent environmental organizations call the programs to task for not demonstrating their effectiveness.

At the end of the day, we meet our zodiac at the beach by the lighthouse. One by one, with help from the lighthouse keeper, we scramble from seaweed-draped rocks over the giant tubular orange sides of the pitching boat. On the ride home, Fairbarns teaches me how to "post," crouching above the seat so that the impact from the giant waves is absorbed by our legs, rather than slamming up through our backs. The boat soars off the top of each second or third wave and seems to hang, spellbound, for a brief moment before crashing down into the trough of the next swell. When we are in the bowl of each wave, we lose sight of the island and the coast of Vancouver Island. We lose sight of everything, in fact, except the next wall of water coming to meet us.

*

MARCH 27, 2011, UNMOORED

> *White fawn lily*
> *Indian plum*
> *Spring gold*
> *Oregon grape*
> *Snowberry leaf out*
> *Licorice fern unravel*
> *Ocean spray leaf out*
> *Spring grass green up*

Most of these I see out the window of the car, or in small patches of bush as I run by a vestige meadow in the evenings. The Matson Lands, Oaklands, Oak Bay, Beacon Hill, West Song Walkway. The days are now longer than the nights. There are days of warm wind, then days of east wind and rain. My friend Nick takes me to his secret Garry oak spot, on the condition that I not name it here. Amidst the high rocky outcrops, earth in the small pockets of moss and grass is soaking and warm; vernal pools shine during brief spells of sun. From the top, we can see 360 degrees, from the heft of Mount Baker and the stretch of the peninsula, around Trial Island's rocky shores and current passes, across McNeil Bay and down the coast to the city, the old water tower a rounded beacon in Rockland. First Nations, he tells me, once used this outcrop as a lookout spot when hunting for whales. We clamber around the six acres. There are hidden patches of licorice fern, hollows perfect for summer night star-gazing, and everywhere dogs off leash. I am a happy clam. Someone has experimented with removing the thorny gorse that car-

pets the park's upper reaches. In one restored area, camas leaves are already crowding in on the bared ground. We walk back through small, wiry oaks that look more like bonsai bushes than full-fledged trees. The sour-spring smell of Indian plum wafts around us. Two white-crowned sparrows fill the grove with their buzzy, floating song, tossed back and forth across the path above our sunlit heads.

Irvin Banman, at the Cowichan Preserve's annual open house.

The Cowichan Garry Oak Preserve

In a climate-modelling project displayed at the Royal BC Museum in 2007 by Biodiversity BC, conservative evaluations estimated that by 2080 the lower third of BC will support only grassland species. If these predictions turn into a reality, and most of the south coast can no longer sustain large populations of conifers, Garry oaks and their associated species may be one of the last native ecosystems that can survive the drought that global warming brings. Creations of refugia, then, are an effective way to help ensure the survival of what may become our only remaining native forests.

In addition to Trial Island, there are a few such refugia, called

The Cowichan Preserve's nursery provides native plant stock to repopulate its meadows.

reserves or preserves, which house extensive Garry oak ecosystems in the Georgian Basin. Only two of these — the Cowichan and Somenos preserves — contain examples of the deep-soil ecosystem described earlier in this book. Perhaps none is so well known or receives as much care as the Cowichan Garry Oak Preserve, just outside of Duncan.

Called the flagship property of the Cowichan Valley by its owner, the Nature Conservancy of Canada, the Cowichan Preserve is an excellent example of high intensity restoration that is pioneering new methods of care. At 21 hectares, the preserve was purchased by the conservancy in 1999, and is perhaps the most intact deep-soil Garry oak ecosystem on the south island. The previous owners, the Elkingtons, were settlers who acquired 600 acres in the 1800s and kept much of it untouched as an oak park, primarily for their own pleasure. The preserve includes many acres of Garry oak meadow that have never been used for cultivation. Though a plethora of groups have done research on the grounds, the property is stewarded mainly by the conservancy's Tim Ennis and Irvin Banman, the site's caretaker. Ennis is based in Victoria and manages land conservation across BC; Banman is centred only on

Cowichan — he lives in the 100-year-old farmhouse at the edge of the property, where Gerald Elkington was born in 1899 and died 105 years later.

Banman's nurseries cover perhaps a quarter acre of the property. Here, one can find deltoid balsamroot, the woolly, glowing sunflower I have otherwise seen only on Mount Tzouhalem, and chocolate-tipped parsley, growing easily and haphazardly in black planters protected by deer fencing. Compost piles are strung along the path. Native grasses poke out from small plugs, lined up neatly in the spring sun. When I visit in May, Banman is using a pair of tweezers to remove invasive species from seedling trays full of native grasses. Each sprout is the thickness of embroidery thread, but propels out of the humus like a green firework. When he is finished ridding the natives of the invaders, Banman repopulates small sections of the preserve, one grass plug at a time. By giving native species a head start in the nursery, he hopes to better foster the survival of dozens of wildflower species that used to thrive in these meadows. Through conversion of patches from European grasses to more delicate native grasses, flowers such as camas, shooting stars and fawn lilies will receive more space and light to bloom and re-seed. It's painstaking work: a hundred green threads fill a two-inch square of meadow, and it's an effort not usually undertaken in restoration projects: native flowers will still bloom amid European grasses, and most sites don't have such a dedicated, full-time steward.

The Cowichan preserve is home to a number of listed species, and research is conducted there by five universities from Canada and the United States. Volunteer efforts are extensive. Plant species are also obtained through plant salvage — the preserve is surrounded on almost all sides by subdivisions, where "Kentucky bluegrass ecosystems," as Ennis dismissively calls lawns, are taking the place of oak meadows. When a developer receives approval to build another subdivision, NCC tries to build relationships in order to rescue whatever native plants can be transplanted. Banman is also experimenting with using sheep to forage on invasive species.

The Cowichan preserve's nurseries were started in 2003 with a few cold frames. Created soil enhances microbes; seed collection from wild populations helps provide nursery stock. In 2011,

Banman was growing 45 species of grasses, wildflowers, trees and shrubs. It's important, he tells me, to provide seed from the local area — biologists have warned him against transplanting oaks or acorns from areas as close as Victoria; there are genetic differences between the trees that, though small, could result in unforeseen consequences.

No other site on Vancouver Island or the Gulf Islands quite compares to either the Cowichan preserve or the nearby Mount Tzouhalem Ecological Reserve, in terms of attention to detail, number of ongoing research projects and resources available for restoration. Perhaps because of the attention granted to them, there are also fierce philosophical battles over what constitutes the right method of restoration within their boundaries. Nowhere is this battle more polarized than on the slopes of Mount Tzouhalem.

Mount Tzouhalem Ecological Reserve

Almost as soon as I enter the world of ecological restoration, I run into a nest of problems that are especially contentious when considering Garry oak ecosystems. How, ask ecologists, botanists, biologists, environmentalists and anthropologists, do we assist in restoring these meadows in an appropriate way? Which species should most thoroughly be protected? What is the intent of the restoration and how should it take place? What will be the final use of a meadow? Will the land be subject to human-centred priorities or nature-centred ones? Do we cut broom or pull it? Do we remove European grasses, or simply add native wildflowers to their mix? And do we remove just invasives, or also other native species that threaten the integrity of an open meadow? Add to this the history of First Nations's longstanding relationships with Garry oak meadows, and their cultivation of the ecosystem over hundreds of generations, and complex problems arise. They are not solved easily, and at colloquia, conferences, universities and non-profits across the south island, there is constant debate. Essentially, to think of restoration, we are forced to consider not just how it should take place, but in whose image it should be made. As ecologist Dave Polster said during our walk at Mount Tzouhalem, when we restore an ecosystem we are always playing God; to move forward, we must admit this, and somehow decide how to get on with the work.

The Tzouhalem Reserve is on the west slope of the mountain, and overlooks Quamichan Lake and the Cowichan Valley's farms and fields. Tzouhalem was named after a Cowichan band member who died in 1859. Originally called Cowichan Mountain, in stories its slopes provided shelter during the Great Flood. Tzouhalem was made into an ecological reserve in 1984, thanks largely to the efforts of Syd Watts and his wife Emily, who worked with the Cowichan Valley Naturalists Society from 1979 onward to save the meadows. Upon creation of the reserve, Watts was appointed volunteer warden of the site; he remains so to the present day. On three sides of the Tzouhalem reserve, the oversized houses of a new subdivision crowd its borders. Almost every home has a commanding view of the island's interior mountain range, but there are few oaks to be seen in their gardens.

Polster leads me from the peak's parking lot through the mountain's Douglas fir forest, where mountain bikers and joggers zoom by, and then along an incongruous chain link fence. This, he tells me, is where the reserve begins; the fence keeps people from creating new trails. A gap appears with a hairpin curve entrance; we go through, over the edge of the ridge and down into the undulating slopes. Mount Prevost rises in front of us, and the rural valleys of Quamichan stretch in pale green waves far below. In the far distance, we can see the snow-covered peaks of the interior range. We walk down past the "trail closed" sign; the path fades, then disappears.

Tzouhalem is perhaps the most untouched oak ecosystem of any I visit on the south island. Sid Watts estimates that 600 hours alone was spent ridding the land of invasive broom plants. Thanks to this work, in May, wave upon wave of shooting star, camas, spring gold and fawn lily stretch out before us. The fawn lilies are in full bloom, the shooting stars are just beginning. Due to the late spring, full bloom won't happen here for another month. Polster moves through the meadow the way I once saw a monk at St. Peter's Benedictine Monastery move through a buttercup meadow — with great grace, despite his size, and on the balls of his feet, picking each footfall so as to injure as little as possible. He takes me down through hollows of fern and small oaks, out to the fringes of the reserve, then up small ravines to look for del-

Deltoid balsamroot (Balsamorhiza deltoidea) in bloom on Mount Tzouhalem, Duncan.

toid balsamroot, a listed species that looks, in bloom, like a grey-and-green leafed, wild and lolling sunflower. He stops and points at a fuzzy bundle of leaves, about two inches from my foot. "We should probably get out of here," he smiles.

Polster's restoration project, to reduce native species encroachment in the meadow, is the source of great controversy on Mount Tzouhalem. A Garry oak meadow is a sub-category of the larger Douglas fir ecosystem on the south coast. When a meadow is not managed by fire to keep it clear and open, native species such as Douglas fir and broadleaf maple begin to encroach on the habitat. For some scientists, encroachment is seen as natural progression of a Garry oak ecosystem subcategory into a dominant Douglas fir forest. Each year, fir seedlings reach further into clearings, drowning out listed species like the yellow montane violet, deltoid balsamroot and white-top aster, which tend to congregate on the edges of the Garry oak/Douglas fir interface. 100 years of fire suppression, coupled with logging in the 1930s and 1940s, has hastened fir encroachment. As the coniferous canopy expands, it creates a darker forest. The open meadow flowers and oaks disappear under shade and the entire area is slowly transformed.

In 2010, the preservation society, with approval from the provincial government, decided to do something about the encroachment. As the advising scientist, Polster prescribed the removal of Douglas fir down to a density that equaled that of the old growth stumps in the area. Smaller trees were limbed as high as Polster and his volunteers could reach with a pole saw and girded. Larger trees were girded and left to decay standing, as he realized that adding a great deal of woody biomass to the forest floor wouldn't help the flower population either. The resulting landscape, he posited, would be somewhat shaded, and thus moister than the open upland meadows, but would let in enough sun to allow the flowers to flourish.

Polster's project, however, argue BC biologists Peter Arcese and Adolf Ceska, fails to provide a baseline comparison for monitoring the success of their efforts. "How," asks Arcese, "will we know how these efforts have measured up in comparison to doing nothing?" In other words, there is no benchmark, no control group used to compare to the areas he has altered. If intervention had to happen, Arcese and Ceska argue, Polster should have divided the area into equal portions, treated half of them and left half untouched, then watched to see where, and if, listed species reappeared.

Another argument against his project is the traditional intent of ecological reserves. Originally created by the federal and provincial governments, reserves were areas that would not see interference from humans. They were seen as places to fence and leave unmolested, regardless of the changes that might naturally take place within their borders. The only justifiable alteration was the removal of invasive species. Otherwise, the land was meant to act as a baseline ecosystem, where the effects of climate change and natural process could be observed unimpeded.

There are a number of problems with this model. For one, the provincial head of Ecological Reserves publicly resigned in 1987, when budgets were slashed dramatically and directors were essentially left in a management role, without any staff to manage. This left a department holding large amounts of land, but with no money to monitor the changes taking place within each ecosystem. Reserves were still reserves, but no data was collected, essentially rendering them silent from a research perspective. Since that time, reserves have been managed by a series of dedi-

Girded Douglas fir on the slopes of Mount Tzouhalem.

cated caretakers, who sometimes live on the land they steward. But this dedication, says Arcese, can also encourage a sense, if not exactly of ownership, then a deep, abiding interest. This interest, of which some consider Polster's project an example, sometimes translates into decision-making that alters the original intent of the preserve.

We are slowly learning the extent to which Garry oak meadows were created and maintained through human participation. Deep- and shallow-soil meadows were also never managed with the idea of rigorous scientific method in mind. Before European contact, they were seen as part of the fabric and body of a culture itself, meant for the mutual benefit of both the people that lived on them and the species that inhabited them. Arcese, however, demurred when asked why a historically culturally managed meadow should now be exempt from further management. "We don't know how often these meadows were burned. Or for how long." The evidence, he says, is anecdotal and it doesn't necessarily apply to the upland meadows. Some research suggests that rocky outcrops meadows remained clear on their own, as they support only species which have adapted to drought conditions, in a way that the deep soil meadows have not. Better, he says, to leave these be.

It could be argued, however, that any present day preserve is ultimately an altered space, even if no restoration modifications are undertaken on the land. Changes in habitat are due to factors that reach much wider than the borders of the protected area. Ecosystems alter from a lack of fires, increased grazing, invasive plants and animals, climate change, pollution, rainwater levels and the encroachment of development. Even house sparrows, who arrive with our housing tracts, make a discernible difference to the behaviour and survival capabilities of native bird species within a preserve.

The results of Polster's encroachment project are already noticeable. The pruning and girding took place in fall 2010; the following spring he saw a marked increase in the number of flower shoots coming up underneath the girded and trimmed trees, due mainly, he says, to increased sunlight. I ask him if he has decided to leave some of the firs uncut as a control patch, as Arcese and Ceska have argued, to show what happens if you don't remove the firs to give the oaks more light. Polster smiles, and looks back up the hill, "The problem with a Douglas fir removal project is that it's a pretty heavy hand. When you see people going after fir trees in an ecological reserve with chainsaws, alarm bells go off. They ask, 'Why are you cutting native trees?' But have a walk through Mount Tzouhalem municipal forest, on the other side of the mountain, and you'll see all the Douglas fir control areas you want. There's not an oak tree left."

We have looked at rare species protection, at encroachment, and the potential disappearance of the Garry oak ecosystem as a whole. There may be other reasons, however, that make these meadows so worth our efforts and keep us coming back, with blistered palms and sore backs, for another session of Saturday morning ivy removal or painstaking species counts.

History and Family

I meet Darcy Mathews and his two-year-old son, Arlo, at Cattle Point on a windy day in June. Mathews is a doctoral student at the University of Victoria. His subject is the First Nations burial cairns scattered across Victoria and Metchosin's oak meadows. The cairns were built by the Straits Salish, or Lekwungen, that made their home on the southern tip of Vancouver Island between 1,000 and 1,500 years ago. "I started research at Rocky Point thinking that I'd find maybe 40 or so burial cairns," Mathews tells me. "I've mapped more than 500 so far and I haven't covered the whole area yet." Mathews is not the first person to take an interest in the cairns. In the late 1880s, Franz Boas led explorations in the area, excavating cairns (and often taking their skulls or skeletons with him back to New York) and collecting archaeological evidence and anthropological stories. The Victoria Natural History Society also completed many excavations, and looters uncovered more cairns in hopes of finding valuable artifacts.

Mathews's study of the cairns, in contrast, embodies respect and gentleness. His excavations go no deeper than the vegetation layer that has covered many of the cairns, cutting back bushes, removing grass thatch and scraping away moss to reveal complex arrangements of stones, some of them thousands of pounds in weight, others as small as an apple. His questions, at this point, outnumber any answers. Why are so many of the cairns situated in Garry oak meadows? Why do they appear in circles, ovals or squares? Why were some of the bodies cremated while others (which Boas unearthed) were interred intact? Why were there few or no artifacts to be found with them? Why, as Mathews has noticed, do they tend to be found alongside the natural walkways through a landscape — between higher rocky knolls and lower vernal pools — as though they might be acting as guideposts to the proper way to traverse the land.

The Lekwungen were a society of classes, and it's possible, as Brian Thom has also posited in his writings on burial cairns in the Gulf of Georgia, that only the upper tier of society was buried in these meadows. Alternatively, it could be that the cairns themselves were meant to mark the boundaries of camas plots, and that placement of one's ancestors there could begin to act as proof of ownership. *My family has been buried here for generations; this is my place.* There is no way of knowing for certain. Mathews is also looking at the Indian consumption plant and its range in

Uplands subdivision survey party at a First Nations burial cairn, Victoria, 1906.
PHOTO BY FRANK CYRIL SWANNELL, COURTESY ROYAL BC MUSEUM, BC ARCHIVES IMAGE
NO. I-33651

meadows. The dried seed pods were used as incense, to mark and strengthen the boundary between the living and the dead. It could be, he muses, as we walk through tall grass gone golden in the last two weeks, that the plant's habitat indicates the location of Lekwungen rituals.

As for the cairns themselves, they may also be, if not exactly a product of their environment, then certainly created with assistance from the camas cultivation that went on in their midst. Speaking with Marguerite Babcock in 1967, Straits Salish Christopher Paul describes piling stones "up in a portion of the plot where there were no camas plants growing, and the brush would be piled to one side, left to rot or to be burned." But Mathews has found no piles of discarded stones at the edges of camas fields. It could be, he tells me, that stones for burial cairns were stockpiled and then used. They may also have been carried from one location to another. For Matthews, cairns offer a powerful link between the life that camas provided and the cycle to death in one's family. In Jewish culture, as well, one places a small stone or pebble on the visited graves of loved ones. The stones create story, marking time with objects. *I was here for you; so was this person, and this person.*

What I realize, walking through the meadows and listening to Mathews, is that *story* in a Garry oak meadow is created through the richness of the place; it is also story that makes the place so rich. It is not just the oak wood used as digging sticks, the camas for food and trading, the stones and their arrangements; it is everything, together. The land here is laden with thousands of years of human care, thought and attendance, both before and after life. Mathews lifts his son away from a perfectly squared-off cairn. The Songhees have told him it's not a great idea for kids to hang around the cairns, so when he comes out to do research, he usually leaves his son at home. There is a dapple of oak leaves and sun and wind. Arlo runs and finds a patch of high grass to lie in, to look up from and watch the sky.

'The Lost Art of Seeing'

Almost a century ago Rainer Maria Rilke poetically hypothesized in his Duino Elegies that it was the earth's destiny to become invisible, that a process of transmutation of the visible into the invisible had begun to take place.... [The] wholesale desertion of the visible world...is part of that fateful story. It's not that the world is any less visible than it was in the past; rather its plenitude registers with us less and less. It is in us that the transmutation takes place .... The basic inability to see a garden in its full-bodied presence is the consequence of a historical metamorphosis of our mode of vision, which is bound up with our mode of being. For as our mode of being changes, so too does our way of seeing.

— ROBERT POGUE HARRISON, *Gardens:*
An Essay on the Human Condition

APRIL 9, 2011, MOUNT TZOUHALEM RESERVE

On the northwest slopes of Mount Tzouhalem, juncos everywhere. Flitting in the branches, scuffing over the moss, darting through the air, their white tail feathers gleaming. Wind rises up from Cowichan Valley and Quamichan Lake and the firs at the edge of the oak grove rush and bend. I am sitting on a small patch of moss, hollowed out, quiet. It's the only spot I have been able to find that is without a blanket of shooting stars. A turkey vulture rises on thermals, crossing from one end of the preserve to the other in a little under half a minute. There is no broom here, no ivy. Only a pelt of moss, grasses and wildflowers, most not yet in bloom. When the sun appears at the hill's east shoulder, the activity of bees, flies and birds notches up a level, and the whole hillside begins to sing. I find myself wondering if, when the hill's millions of camas flowers open in May, the slope will turn a blue so rich it might be visible from the valley below.

Robert Pogue Harrison argues that our civilization's gardens (and indeed the entire visible world) are being lost to us because our ability to apprehend the world has been curtailed by the effects of modern life. We live at a frenzied pace. Our lives, based largely in the virtual, leave little room for the time needed to experience gardens as they were originally designed: "places of self-discovery, of spiritual cultivation, of personal transformation." Without the space and time to see a Garry oak meadow, or a garden such as Ryoanji Zen in Kyoto, with its half-buried stones and expanses of raked gravel, or the English gardens of Stowe, a garden's depths cannot "unfold its appearances" for the viewer. "Time in its subjective and objective correlates is the invisible element in which gardens come to bloom."

For many of us who visit a Garry oak meadow but once every few weeks, taking an afternoon, for example, to hike from parking lot through its midst on the way to the sea — as one can do at Devonian Regional Park — our time in the meadows is usually limited to moments. Even if we do pause to take in the view of a spring bloom, we are still on our way to elsewhere, whether physically or mentally. We have come to a point in history where "there is much that we are no longer able to see today in the visible world" because "the inner gaze needed to apprehend it is either

obscured or directed elsewhere." We think of the end of the trail.
We chalk up the tasks that must be accomplished in the rest of the
day. We can even check our email from the peak. Even if we stop
to take in the colours in a meadow and appreciate its flowers, often
our concentrated efforts to see result only in the "impossibility of
accessing its spiritual transcendence."

If time and space are both needed in order to allow a garden, or a
meadow, to unfold all of its significance, then who, oddly, does get
to attend to these places with a regularity and quietness of attention
that can breed not just sight but seeing? It is those who spend time
not just passing through but participating in the life of a garden
who perceive it not as a representation, but as a phenomenon. As
gardeners, we must cut the branch, pull the weed, shape the look
and feel of a landscape. We must participate. As caretakers, we
spend hours tending and restoring the land, removing those species that do not fit and tending into health those that do. In these
meadow gardens, we often work at one small task, repetitively,
obsessively, and over the length of the day, find that our manner of
seeing, and indeed our entire mode of being, slows to the pace at
which these gardens unfold. Once again, care becomes the manner by which we are allowed entry into this world of true perception. If a Garry oak meadow is a garden, its humming expanse
requires "a willingness to linger and a readiness for thought that
our present frenzy finds abhorrent." Thus can these places come
to our rescue, drawing us out of ourselves and helping us to relearn
"the art of seeing," making the invisible visible again.

Madronamai: In Praise of Oaks

Off island, out of country, on an ancient riverbed turned glacial-
till alluvial floodplain, is Madronamai Nursery, about 10 miles east
of the I5, just after crossing the Canadian border. Surrounded by
the Two Sisters Mountains, Mount Baker and Sumas Mountain,
Madronamai is bucolic on an Indian summer day. Row upon row
of Garry oaks sit in the gold and green fields. The grass gives off its
heated summer smell; footsteps sound a dry rasp in the recording
I make of my walk with owner Philip Marble. A bearded, bright-
eyed man, a gentle talker, Marble has stewarded Garry oaks from
seed to tree for more than 25 years. As we walk through the straight

rows of the oak groves, he gazes into the distance at the light, as if taking in the geometry of his trees and their beauty but giving them the courtesy of a look askance.

Marble operates Madronamai as the sole nursery in the northwest that offers mature Garry oaks for landscaping projects. The trees are sold to landscapers as far south as California and up to British Columbia. Many have trunks a foot in diameter. They stretch 30 feet into the air and have the look of sprawling, deep-soil oaks. To manage them, he maintains the root ball using stitched burlap and through periodic root pruning. Most of Marbles' trees are purchased by construction contractors or landscape architects, as well as state funded park projects. Many have ended up on the San Juan Islands. To transport a tree from Madronamai to Comox, where some of his specimens ended up a few years ago, *Philip Marble* costs about $1,400. The trees themselves cost several thousand *in his oak* more. When needed, he hires a team of labourers, hand-digs four *tree nursery,* or five feet around the root ball and, using a huge fork lift, plucks *Madronamai,* the young trees from the ground like giant carrots and loads them *Washington* onto a flatbed. *State.*

For some, Garry oaks are inseparable from their meadows. The fawn lilies of the lowlands, sea blush of the rocky cliffs and cliff swallows that inhabit the pastures are as important and beautiful as the trees themselves. Marble admires every aspect of the natural world, but his love for the oaks is unparalleled. We crisscross back and forth between his grove of young trees and the mature oaks. It's October, but the leaves have not yet begun turning, and it's so green and warm it could be high summer. Marble's stories are triggered by the sight of a jawbone in the soil, or some branch or shape that catches his eye. Foremost in his anecdotes is his dedication to form over function. He describes becoming entranced by a variety of penstemon seen when mountain climbing in the 1980s in Washington's coast range, the delicacy of the flowery perennial's growing pattern in rock. His climbing partner ripped one out in order to anchor a belay point, and he watched in grief as it sailed down the cliff.

After this story, there's no need to ask why he chose oaks, the slowest growing of any deciduous tree on the coast, from which to make his living. Always, there is an overarching sense of the space the trees occupy in air, the regular rows, the irregular reach of each limb. We both agree there is a beauty in the winter branch that rivals its summer appearance. When sorting through photos of his grove later that winter, the calligraphy of the branches recalls, with amazing similarity, that same chaotic regularity of an olive grove. To Adam Zagajewski, the order of the rows and the disorder of the branches created a third space, one he called the "olive tree of nothingness." It may be this space, a *negative blue* defined by the sculpture of oak branches amidst light, wind and birds, that Marble regularly calls to praise.

APRIL 26, 2011 BEACON HILL PARK

At the Easter break I interrupt my weekly routine with the oaks for four days in Tofino. When I depart, it is at the end of two straight months of cold rain and snow. When I return four days later, it is spring. My dog and I walk the cliffs of Dallas road and Checkerboard Hill, both of us euphoric. On the windward side of the hill, the oaks are still closed, but on the lee side, their leaves have begun to unfurl. This process defies the most careful attempt at observation, as it seems to happen in sepia, as if in an old film. Garry oaks, when they first unfurl, are not green. They are saffron, copper, rust, yolk, gold or fire. They are furry as the underside of your childhood guinea pig, and just as bright orange. For one terrifying instant I think I have missed it, the key moment of growth I've been waiting for all spring. Then, with the dog bounding alongside camas that is beginning to open, I realize I have arrived just in time.

Beauty

In summer's early dusk, long grasses in the oak meadow at Beacon Hill turn a glowing ochre that painters say reflects the most light of any shade. Many artists undercoat their paintings with this hue in order to lend a greater luminosity to their work. The ochre in a meadow also shines in this luminous way. Dragonflies knit the air above the grass. Song sparrow, red-tailed hawk, mason bee, bumble bee, tree swallow, bush tit, raccoon, Anna's hummingbird; all of these make their home here and lend a vividness to the scene. The grass is touched by wind; heat rises from the fields.

When we speak of beauty, philosopher Elaine Scarry says, we note three things. First, there is the beautiful object itself. The meadow at Beacon Hill at dusk, for instance, has a clarity of colour which stretches into the distance. It has symmetry in the vertical line of the grasses and the horizontal bands of clouds that sit against the sky. It has unity in both the visual picture it creates and in the interdependence of species that make their home in it. The Romantic poet Gerard Manley Hopkins wrote that our sense of beauty is one in which regularity and irregularity, symmetry and non-symmetry are intertwined. Beauty is a relation of things: grasses under the occasional tree; bands of cloud against a mostly clear sky; the whorl and twist of an oak limb; stillness and wind.

Being Pierced and Being Happy About It

Sometimes, says Scarry, when we speak of beauty we are not talking about the object itself (in this case, the meadow) but about the response it elicits in us. Two things happen when we apprehend beauty: the immediate response and the enduring response. The immediate response is unmistakable: we step onto the path that

A pile of removed Scotch broom on Mount Tzouhalem.

leads through the meadow and we are arrested, stopped in our tracks by the unmistakable and sharp sensory pleasure it elicits. As in the comprehension of a metaphor in poetry, we are struck. Poet and philosopher Jan Zwicky would call this being "pierced." The particularity, the *"this*ness" of the meadow steps out and hits us over the head: we are left speechless. As the poet Tim Lilburn writes, "everything exceeds its name"; we are dumbed into a state of awe.

The immediate moment of beauty, as when we step into the meadow, involves, as Iris Murdoch writes, an "unselfing." Scarry calls this a state of "opiated adjacency." We are made marginal, as if sidelined. We realize we are not the centre of the world. We see something other than us and see it entirely; as Simone Weil writes, this beautiful thing acts like small tears in the surface of the world that pull us through to some vaster space." It is a radical decentering. Beauty, Scarry says, is the only thing that can divert attention from us, and simultaneously makes us content to be sidelined. "We willingly cede our ground to the thing that stands before us."

To cede ground means to admit to being only one of many species on earth, ceding dominance and becoming protectors rather than destroyers. When it comes to our remaining oak meadows, and to the tiny plots we tend in our yards, to admit we have seen beauty in a wild oak landscape is to come face to face with that responsibility to care, to tend as gardeners of the earth.

Replication

The third part of apprehending our meadow occurs in those enduring moments after we have viewed it, and involves, Scarry writes, a desire to replicate. Wittgenstein writes that "when the eye sees something beautiful, the hand wants to draw it." Our urge is to grasp the wrist of the person next to us and point. It is to photograph, to sketch, to keep it in sight. The clamouring of the world arrests us and leads us to replication of the beautiful thing. In re-creation — through story, painting or physical restoration of our meadow — we enlarge and multiply the world; in so doing, we multiply beauty as well.

The opposite of beauty, to Scarry, is not ugliness, but injury, which shares its root with the word injustice. The tendency towards replication, or creation, when confronted with an ochre-coloured meadow on a warm evening in August, takes us away from inclination to injure and back towards care. "Beauty makes us eligible not only to look at the things that seize our attention, but makes us eligible to go on and be caring about other objects as well, and the same thing can be said of persons."

Beauty is a call for us to create something better, to protect that which has pierced us and elicited our desire to stop and attend. For when we stop, we enter into a "compact, or contract" with the beautiful thing. "Beauty seems to place requirements on us for attending to the aliveness...of our world, and for entering into its protection." The beauty of the ochre coloured meadow in late August is as important a feature as its astounding biodiversity. It must be held as dear as the listed species we shepherd from seed to flower. Beauty calls on us to be better, to tend to things well. The compact or contract we make includes this pleasurable obligation, the same that one binds the fox to the little prince; that binds Odysseus to Penelope, that binds all of us to our loves.

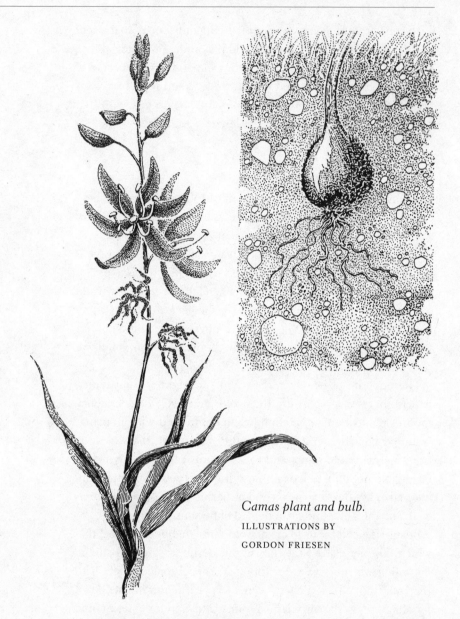

Camas plant and bulb.

ILLUSTRATIONS BY
GORDON FRIESEN

The response that a beautiful landscape triggers as well as the call to treat it well were ways of living ingrained into the culture and fabric of First Nations life, which may be why they use the term beautiful so infrequently when speaking of Garry oak meadows. "My parents never told me they loved me when I was growing up," a Liard elder told indigenous rights lawyer Drew Mildon during land negotiations. "We were part of them, like we were part of the land. It wasn't necessary to say." Aesthetics and value was firmly tied to the utility and spiritual, physical and emotional power inherent in a land; to call it beautiful would be to call attention to oneself as beautiful — in a healthy culture, it was a firmly held belief unnecessary to voice.

Clayton George's experience of spoken and unspoken understandings is similar. George, of the Cowichan Nation, gives a talk on traditional uses of the meadows at the Cowichan Garry Oak Preserve, including the history of his childhood out on the land, learning the Hul'qumi'num names for medicinal and food plants from his family. When I ask him about the idea of the beauty of the meadows, however, he pauses on the trail, and defers first to Tim Ennis, of the Nature Conservancy. "Tim talked about the beauty of the meadows, but I've never heard that idea from our perspective. I just heard my grandparents talk about living off the land and working together."

Coast Salish could complete the work needed to sustain themselves in far less time than interior First Nations communities. The weather was clement and food was plentiful. According to Daniel Marshall, the Cowichan tribes had "dominant control over two of the most important salmon-spawning rivers flowing into the Strait of Georgia — the Cowichan and Fraser." Some put the number of weekly hours needed to complete basic survival tasks at approximately 12. A 12-hour work week leaves a great deal of time for artistic and cultural development, as well as to appreciate the aesthetic pleasures of a meadow in which one is digging one's food.

A Garry oak meadow is, finally, a meeting ground, an alternate space where two cultures find themselves cherishing the same patch of ground, but often for different reasons. The commonality of aesthetic experience and value stretches between these two communities and between past and present, creating a cultivated space, a garden where attention and care are key to entry and understanding.

Gardeners

Knowledge is always situated.
It's where one perfects.
Thinking lives.
No waste of work, no waste of time.

— LYN HEJINIAN, *The Language of Inquiry*

MAY 30, 2011, UPLANDS PARK

In the midst of Uplands Park's camas meadow, Margaret Lidkea is searching for her secateurs. Her hair falls forward as she bends and parts the grass. Lidkea is a volunteer with Friends of Upland Park and the Oak Bay Parks department. The park logs the hours that volunteers put in and receives matching funding for Garry oak ecosystem restoration projects. With the funds, it hires students for summer work projects and to aid in removal of invasive species. Lidkea has been working with the municipality of Oak Bay and Girl Guides of Canada since 1993, and the meadow in which we meet is known as Guide Meadow. Each year she works to rid a larger area of broom and gorse and runs education programs for children through both volunteer groups and her previous job with the Swan Lake Nature Sanctuary. The trails through the meadows are so muddy, she tells me, because the Uplands park manager has chosen not to bring in wood chips or other foreign materials that might change the soil composition.

It is this dark, rich, thick soil that I first notice on entering the park. It looks nothing like the acidic gravel that I used to garden in the Highlands; nor is it like the clay-based fill that surrounds so many residential houses in the city. It looks as if it were meant for growing, and the verdant conditions are testament. Native haw-thorne rises around us in the rocky meadows, and there are 22 spe-cies at risk found within the park, including seven listed species. In the drier sites, the camas has passed its peak by May's end, but in the vernal pools to which we walk, where higher water tables delay growth, great and common camas, buttercup and lupine are in full bloom. It is less extensive, yes, than in Sir James Douglas's day, but still akin to the surface of a summer lake — the colour sinks into my chest and begins to hum.

There are hundreds of people across southern Vancouver Island and the Gulf Islands, not to mention from the San Juan Islands south to the coast of California, working on the restoration of Garry oak ecosystems. Almost every park that contains an oak in the Capital Region has a society or "friends of" group, most staffed by volunteers who give up their time to remove invasive species and shepherd the health of oaks and native plants. Bluebird rein-troduction projects, like the one on San Juan Island, install nest boxes built by inmates in nearby prisons and band and monitor nesting pairs. The philosophies for present-day management and the goals for future survival of oak ecosystems can be found in the stories of these people and their dedication, or even, as I learned the hard way, their attempts.

Irvin Banman

To step into the Cowichan Garry Oak Preserve in September is to slip into a world of copper. Leaves of the oaks in the lower water table areas have already gone brown and gold. The grass is spun straw and the slanted light of late summer drifts through the can-opy.

Irvin Banman has prepared the site before the arrival of 10 other volunteers, including participants from BC Parks, Parks Canada and Nature Conservancy Canada. Kate Proctor and I drive up from Victoria. Proctor is completing her master's thesis using

Burning the meadows, Cowichan Garry Oak Preserve, Duncan.

research plots in the preserve, studying responses to fire by the preserve's plant species. We arrive just as the team has begun soaking the mowed perimeter of the first burn with fire hoses, which bring water from Lake Quamichan, almost a kilometre away. Using a Tiger torch, Banman lights the first fire while his crew stands ready on either side, hoses running. The day is almost windless, sunny and warm, and the fall rains are predicted to begin tomorrow. Perfect conditions, in other words, for a meadow fire.

Together with researcher Andrew MacDougall of Guelph University, Banman has been key to restoring the natural process of fire to the Cowichan Preserve. He began burning the meadows using one-metre-square test patches in 1999. A wet plywood box was laid over a square of meadow and the perimeter was soaked and then covered in wet blankets. Usually, there was so much surrounding moisture that test patches had to be burned entirely by Tiger torch. With help from Oregon State University and a five-year research project, municipal restrictions were lightened and the conservancy began burning five-metre-square parcels, then by 2007 its first larger-scale burns. By 2011, after a decade of burning,

Banman has earned enough trust from local fire protection officials and the community to complete several 300- to 500-square-
metre burns in the preserve.

During a burn, the surface and air temperature of a grass fire can
reach hundreds of degrees, but the soil temperature may rise less
than one degree, which is key to stimulating the growth of native
plants. Burning also reduces the thatch that grasses build up over
time and makes it easier for native wildflowers to get the sun and
moisture they need. Banman's fire drifts out from its starting point
in a calm semi-circle, advancing up the slope against the wind at
a few feet a minute. When it meets the edge of the mowed area,
it peters out with a sizzle. Occasionally, a larger patch of orchard
grass will send the flames as high as six feet and speed the fire's
progress, but mostly, there is a lovely calmness to both the fire's
progression and to the group's management, as they reinforce the
perimetre with hoses and watch for drifting sparks. They talk and
take photos; Banman smiles from the far side of the clearing, a
wall of flame between him and the lens.

Burned meadow grass falls beautifully as carbon in the same
pattern as its windswept, pre-burned state. The black swirls and
waves, almost immediately cool to the touch, will disintegrate
under the first rain, leaving white ash, which will also disappear
within a month beneath a bolt of new growth. Banman looks out
over the blackened field. "I'd like to work up to burning a tenth of
this land every year," he says. We crouch down where the line of
burned grass meets the unburned meadow. There is a shelf of perhaps two inches, where gold falls away to black. Banman brushes
away the carbon; the living moss underneath it — green, moist,
thriving — bends under his touch.

Roberta McCarthy

In June, I spend an afternoon in Roberta McCarthy's garden in
Oak Bay with Carolyn Masson from GOERT. We are here to view
Roberta's camas meadow, which she has let develop over the last
twenty-six years, since the land's original estate was strata-divided
and the sprawling, deep-soil meadows became home to 10 residences. The estate's original stone house still stands down the private lane, where a treaty tree (a tree which is said to have served as

a negotiation site between tribes) digs into the ground and sprouts out again from two separate trunks. The lawn around the stone house is manicured and antiseptic but at the McCarthy's the back garden stretches to the road in an unbroken wave of long grasses, oaks, great camas and chocolate lily.

Roberta grew up in Victoria. She seems to be half plant, graciously and quietly drifting through her yard, touching the edges of leaves and poking at the ground, then rising to offer us tea. "It's amazing what you've done here," I say and she corrects me gently, "No, it's really what I haven't done that has made a difference." The first spring she arrived in the house her husband, who likes a well-kept yard, was fortuitously away; she passed hours watching the entire yard sprout waves of shooting stars, camas then chocolate lilies. She has attended this unfolding every year since that first season, and every summer after the bloom she collects the seeds, cuts the grass short and scatters the seeds. McCarthy volunteers at nearby Anderson hill, pulling broom, ivy and the piles of gorse I saw earlier this spring. She also combs the commons of the strata, clipping ivy from the bases of oaks and encouraging oak seedlings to sprout in her husband's more manicured front garden. She is a dream landowner, worrying about the health of the oaks and practising her own form of management by limbing the maples to let light in, and by taking camas and Erythronium seeds to scatter in nearby oak parks. She invites us to come back anytime. On the way home, gentle, girlish Carolyn tells me the story of Masanobu Fukuoka, the author of *One Straw Revolution*, which advises: dig less, scatter more seeds.

The San Juan Island Preservation Trust

Gardeners do more than tend the earth. Since moving to the city I have noticed how insects, birds and other wildlife flock to those properties where trees and native plants are permitted to thrive. Western bluebirds are particularly vulnerable to the loss and fragmentation of habitat. Extirpated from the Southern Gulf Islands, the San Juans and Vancouver Island for decades, bluebirds prefer an open grassland habitat and typically use Garry oaks to provide their cavity nesting sites. With fewer oaks left to decay naturally, the birds lose nesting habitat and cannot maintain breeding

populations. Their disappearance is also due to pesticide use and predation by house sparrows, common starlings, crows, cats and raccoons. Before the advent of the Western Bluebird Reintroduction Program, the last breeding pair on San Juan was noted more than 40 years ago. The last known pair on Vancouver Island was seen in 1995. On San Juan Island, remnant Garry oak meadows and tall grass pastureland have provided, through the generous support of private landowners, an opportunity to recreate a garden full of birds.

A San Juan Preservation Trust Western bluebird nest box, San Juan Island, WA.

The bluebird project has operated on San Juan Island since 2006, and 2011 marked the final year of phase one of the project. According to the American Bird Conservancy, during the five-year project, the San Juan Island Preservation Trust, in cooperation with Bob Altman of the Conservancy, "captured and translocated 45 breeding pairs from expanding populations at the Fort Lewis Military installation, Washington, and another four pairs from the Willamette Valley in Oregon." Nesting boxes are installed by volunteers and monitored for breeding populations. During the program's tenure, 212 fledglings were produced, and as of 2011, the island had 15 breeding pairs of birds, which fledged 74 birds. In 2012, 13 returning pairs had been sighted by early May. The fledge rate during the tenure of the program was, amazingly, the same as Fort Lewis's.

The San Juan program is notable for a few reasons. Songbird reintroduction is challenging: bluebirds will leave for migration at the end of every summer season and there's never any guarantee they'll return in subsequent years. The San Juan project is also the only reintroduction program to occur entirely on private land and be funded by private donations, which meant that the cooperation of landowners was required for placement of aviaries, nest box installation and monitoring.

Perhaps most importantly for Garry oak meadows in southern BC, the Garry Oak Ecosystems Recovery Team is now replicating the San Juan project in the Cowichan Garry Oak preserve in Duncan, with the preservation trust's assistance. At a bluebird celebration on San Juan on a golden September afternoon, Altman handed over the first honorary nest box to Kathryn Martell, Conservation Specialist with GOERT. The box was made, as were many of the 600 on San Juan, by inmates at the Stafford Creek Corrective Center in Washington State; the box given to Martell was constructed by inmate 496. She peeked inside, smiling. "Does the box include a pair of bluebirds?"

My Sister's Meadow

Sometimes, to garden is to try to reshape the world a little, and a gardening project can often become as large as one's imagination and desire. Sometimes that desire proves stronger than the garden itself.

As part of the research for this book, and as a way of doing something tangible, I want to recreate a Garry oak meadow on a degraded city lot. After studying maps and drainage patterns and spending too much time standing in my own yard over the winter, I stall by turning to the backyard of my sister, who also lives in Saanich, in an area full of mature oaks. Over a number of conversations in February and March, I convince her to let the top half of her back yard go wild. "You won't have to mow it," I say. "It will be just what your oak needs. You won't have to rake in fall."

"But what about the weeds? What will the neighbours say? They already hate my tree." She peppers me with questions, distrustful, or perhaps just a little incredulous that she can leave a portion of her property to its own devices, more or less, and it will eventually blossom into something beautiful. But she agrees.

In mid-April, I arrive at her house with pots full of camas and oak seedlings, some nodding onion, bunch grass and a shooting star. She nurtures Nootka rose and Indian plum, keeps the snowberry along the back fence and removes the ivy. The meadow develops beautifully — golden and full of wild pea — until August, when the perimeter drainage project she's been planning for, in order to keep her basement dry, turns out to be more expensive than first thought. Over the course of two days, she is presented with and chooses a cheaper solution. The meadow, and all it contains, is bulldozed, the slope reformed and covered with landscaping cloth and bark mulch. I find out after the fact, too late to save the transplants, too late to offer alternatives.

Carolyn Masson, GOERT staff, in the late Patricia Boyle's native plant garden, a stunning example of Garry oak meadow restoration on Gonzales Bay, Victoria.

Garry oak meadow; acrylic on canvas by Victoria artist Jo Roueche.

There is no simple answer to the question of priorities when it comes to caretaking the natural world. We cannot easily tell a single mother to spend an additional four thousand dollars for the sake of a few camas bulbs. Neither, however, can we continue to justify destruction of natural habitat. Until our municipalities present us with choices, however — such as rain gardens as a legitimate alternative to storm sewers, or tax breaks for those who choose to grow native species — we will remain in this bind.

Changing the laws, too, would help change landowner perceptions. My sister, and many other city dwellers, have never been entirely comfortable with the idea of a landscape that needs little tending. Weeding, trimming and managing European species have become such a lexicon for our relationship with our yards that we are reluctant, sometimes even fearful, to invite native species to thrive. To relinquish control is to invite criticism, to risk being called neglectful. And the ultimate trump cards of property value and safety can always be called, however inaccurately, to reinforce critics's arguments.

AUGUST 6, 2011, BEACON HILL PARK

The light is perfect. In a small wind, the grasses below Checkerboard Hill bend at the tips and flash the last of the sun across the fields. Gone are the seed heads of the camas, buried underneath four-foot stems. All around us, golden expanse, dark green oaks, crickets, wind. The sky is indigo in the east, salmon in the west, and the hill is speckled with couples spooning on blankets or just watching the shift from afternoon to dusk. Jo, Maisie and I hover in the field, taking photos. Less than a week later, the city mows the hillside, leaving the chafe in pale yellow swathes on the slopes.

My Meadow

It was April when my sister landscaped her meadow. Come summer, a story unfolds in my own yard. I write with both regret and elation. There exist many homeowners who mow their postage stamps into submission every three days and who consider what is natural to be anathema to proper, neighbourly living. I regret the missed opportunity and those constricted carpets of Kentucky bluegrass, which have come to be seen as beautiful, right and good. My elation, however, comes from the groundswell of support that counteracts, so ardently, these views.

The poet Tim Lilburn once suggested, when writing of the Saskatchewan prairies, that European settlers who had come, homesteaded and raised generations of children had never really landed on the place which they settled. They lived hovering in the air. There was a disconnection between the original landscape, their perceptions and what they pictured in its place. What they found was tall- and short-grass prairie, its wide expanses supporting a host of songbirds, insects and animals. The roots of the prairie grasses were so deeply entrenched in the soil that when the land was first broken by plough, the sound of the roots breaking, so loud and deep, was mistaken for gunshot. What they created — through the first crops of wheat and alfalfa, which took more and more land from the remaining buffalo, to industrial, high-yield agribusiness — was anathema to biodiversity. Of course, they didn't understand. The prairie landscape as it originally appeared before them was essentially invisible. As with the history on this country's west coast, their experience was, and continues to be, primarily one of takeover, alteration and erasure.

In late-spring, I begin to create a meadow in order to bring birds and insects to my yard, to create shade and to mimic a wild landscape like the one in which I had lived in for the previous seven years. By late June, my lawn is two to four feet high and peppered in Garry oak trees only three inches high. When I look out the kitchen window I see a rural Saanich field, all green-golden and wild and shot through with the rose and blue tints of grass seed. Small postage stamp though it is, I am pleased. Apparently, others are not. I receive a letter from Saanich bylaw enforcement, saying that someone has complained about the overgrown look of the yard. I have 10 days to remove the meadow under the "noxious weeds" Bylaw 8080 or they will come and cut it at my expense.

I respond by leaking the story to three local papers and responding to Saanich with a warning against trespass. The next day, I spend all morning trying to get a bylaw officer to answer the phone and finally speak with Bill Storey. "Don't worry," he says, congenially, "We're not going to come and mow your place down immediately." He needs to check with Adriane Pollard in Environmental Services, but he ventures that an exception might also be made for me, as it has been, apparently, for others who argued the case of restoration on their properties; their environmental policies, he reminds me, are there to encourage residents to do just that.

Meanwhile, two papers take an interest, interviewing me and then visiting to take photos. Wanting an audience, my next door neighbour, who I have not yet met, takes the opportunity to shake his finger in my face and the face of the journalist from *Monday Magazine*. He criticizes everything from the pine needles on my driveway to the seedlings. If I don't cut the unruly grass, he warns, he will come over with his lawnmower and do so for me. I glance around at the rosy seed heads shining in the light. When did order trump beauty, I wonder? When did the aesthetics of a

My meadow, with Maisie.
PHOTO BY DANIELLE POPE / MONDAY MAGAZINE

native landscape take a back seat to control? Before the Italians and their pleasure gardens. Before the Greek bowers, the Mesopotamian cultivated fields. All the way back to Eden, and its exactness, which rose above the slovenly wilderness that surrounded its walls.

My neighbour's critique, however, sticks in my mind. Thinking of my impending meeting with Saanich Environmental Services staff Adriane Pollard, I realize none of the seeds that I've scattered will be visible to judging eyes. My intent was to continue to populate the outskirts of the yard with cuttings from Indian plum, red currant and other native bushes, in order to make a native hedgerow, and to plant more oak seedlings as I found them — only 50 percent of the trees I transplanted from a generous resident's property in Saanichton have survived. But I have yet to do this. I head to Russells nursery on the weekend and pillage the place, spending my savings on black hawthorne, Nootka rose, Pacific nine bark, red alder, arbutus and a host of other native plants.

On Saturday morning, I make the front page of the *Times-Colonist*: "Amid tall grasses, tensions grow: gardener ticketed after going native." Here, dear reader, lies elation. Cars and bikes cruise the street, slowing down when they reach my house. Most stop to extend, amazingly, their support. One woman offers to lie down in front of Saanich's lawnmowers, should the need should arise. Others ask if I will start a petition. I receive letters, emails, phone calls of support, as well as gifts on the doorstep, offers of seeds and seedlings or help with restoration work. People write the mayor and blind copy me by email. They site reduced water use, lower levels of noise and air pollution (thanks to fewer lawnmowers), more native habitat and a need to change our notion of what is beautiful and acceptable in suburban areas. As bicyclists ride by and wave, I feel a kinship with my species and a sense of belonging to my community. I feel like my feet are on the ground.

In *Gardeners of Eden* Dan Dagget describes two maps of the continental United States, one showing the duration of human settlement in an area and the other showing which areas had the most threatened and endangered species. The correlation, he writes, was obvious, but surprising. Wherever humans had landed and stayed in stable, resident populations for the longest time, fewer plants and animal species had become endangered. This opposes the views of environmentalists who favour wilderness parks as untouchable refugia for nature. It questions the thinking that to truly care for a place, we must leave it alone.

Adriane Pollard and local fire officials arrive the following week; by Wednesday I have official approval to keep the meadow. Environmental Services and fire department have both agreed that the property poses no risk to surrounding houses. I celebrate by holding an "open meadow" the following weekend. About 75 people pass through, many with their own stories of attempted restoration and the responses they have encountered from neighbours and municipalities. Urban gardening advocates chat with CRD parks restorationists. People bring pictures of their own yards and ask advice on how to care for their oaks. A Saanich councillor drops by to tell me she will bring the issue up at the next parks meeting. In September, I hear from Pollard that several Saanich councillors have voiced their desire to amend the Noxious Weeds Bylaw to accommodate "naturescaping."

Opposition, however, always hovers nearby. Saanich has lost 13 percent of its urban tree canopy in the last 25 years to development and disease. Arborist Ryan Senechal says perhaps one in 100 of the residents he visits know the value of the Garry oaks in their yard and take an interest in native-plant gardening. "The work we would like to do — helping landowners care for their oaks properly — makes up less than a tenth of our business." The majority of his work involves residents who demand pruning of healthy limbs so that they might better view the Olympic Mountains. Senechal is passionate about all trees, but particularly about oaks, and mourns the housing developments, insects and diseases that threaten them. He advocates for greater collaboration between arborists, municipalities and restoration organizations like GOERT. But what he'd really like is to work for more people like Mike and Anne Stack, who own an acre of oak trees near Interurban Road, in Saanich. Instead of cutting down a diseased tree, on Senechal's recommendation the Stacks made it into a wildlife refuge; he limbed the trunk twenty feet high and notched in the beginnings of holes for cavity nesting birds. Their yard is full of snowberry and hundred year old oaks, and the Stacks are now working to create an extensive native plant garden below the limbed oak. Friendship gates on either end of the property allow children to pass through the glade on their way to school; when I visited, she told me she wanted to bequeath their oak forest to the community, "It was my parent's land; it's important to me that these trees continue to thrive for the good of the neighbourhood."

Epilogue

MAY 1, 2012, HOME

This spring, at my request and to my great joy, Saanich Parks staff arrived in a truck and planted a Garry oak tree on my boulevard as part of its Urban Forest Strategy. One of the strategy's major stated concerns is the preservation of Garry oak ecosystems. The tree is six feet tall and sits girded by a wooden stake. Its leaves, in this year's warmer spring, unfolded in late April; I think it is one of the most beautiful things I have ever seen. On condition that I water the tree when necessary, there was no charge for the planting. All Saanich residents with desire for a boulevard tree are eligible to participate in this program; it is also possible to specifically request a native species of tree.

During a visit to Mount Tzouhalem last spring, I asked Dave Polster what the impetus was behind people's desire to save the meadows. We were standing in late morning sun, in the transition zone between oak glade and Douglas fir and arbutus woodland. Last year's leaves lay on the ground, many pierced by the new, green leaves of satin flower and nodding onion. He glanced at me sideways. "Do you want to hear what I think is the real reason, or the answer scientists usually give?" "Both," I smiled.

Officially, he told me, reserves serve as a benchmark for disappearing ecosystems. This answer concerns protection of listed species, halting the decline of nesting rates of endangered birds, preventing the disappearance of species and maintaining reserves as a repository, a sanctuary to show us what our world used to look like. This reason encompasses all the facts that ecologists, botanists, biologists and conservationists know by heart. But, Polster told me, that's not the whole story. "People get a spiritual lift when they enter this ecosystem," continued Polster. "This is critically important to our being able to connect with the land, but too often, this connection isn't given any credence. People feel lost and empty and think that if they buy a bigger TV they're going to find happiness. I don't think so. I think it has to do with caretaking and reconnection and appreciation of beauty. Certainly Garry oak ecosystems are stunningly beautiful. In their pristine condition, you don't have to have much imagination to truly see this."

Here, perhaps, is the crux of this story: we love what is beautiful, as so many have argued. We love what is rare and fleeting. And many of us will work our fingers to the bone to protect what gives us not just physical sustenance, but a sense of emotional or spiritual connection and belonging to the place we live. This book could have been written about my lost Douglas fir and arbutus forest. It could have been written about our urban creeks — Bowker, Millstream, Craigflower — or about the Southern Gulf Islands' aquamarine coves and shell beaches. The feeling is the same. The connection is the same. What we love best chooses us, or we choose it, but there is little difference in the way and the manner in which that love comes alive; there is little difference in the sustenance and beauty inherent in that which is loved.

Appendix

Except where noted, photos in this book are taken by the author. For colour versions, as well as media and links to further reading, please visit www.maleeaacker.com/gardens.

For a comprehensive listing of the species found in Garry oak meadows, as well as details on the listed species found within their realm, the reader is best directed to the Garry Oak Ecosystems Recovery Team's impressive Species at Risk listing, accessible for free at www.goert.ca, or to April Pettinger's comprehensive book, *Native Plants in the Coastal Garden*. The following is a listing of Garry oak meadow plants seen or discussed in this book. Unless otherwise indicated, all listed plants are native species.

Trees
    Garry oak (*Quercus garryana*)
    Douglas fir (*Pseudotsuge meziesii*)
    Arbutus (*Arbutus menziesii*)

Shrubs
    Medium bearberry (*Arctostaphylos X media*)
    Indian plum (*Oemleria cerasiformis*)
    Oceanspray (*Holodiscus dicolor*)
    Oregon grape (*Mahonia nervosa* and *M. aquifolium*)
    Saskatoon (*Amelanchier alnifolia*)
    Snowberry (*Symphoricarpos albus* and *S. mollis*)

Wildflowers
    Small-flowered alumroot (*Heuchera microntha*)
    Western buttercup (*Ranunculus occidentalis*)

Common camas (*Camassia quamash*)
Great camas (*Camassia leichtlinii*)
Meadow death camas (*Zygadenus venenosus*)
Red fescue (*Festuca rubra*)
Fringecup (*Tellima grandiflora*)
Tufted hairgrass (*Deschampsia cespitosa*)
Chocolate lily (*Fritillaria affinis* or *F. lanceolata*)
White fawn lily (*Erythronium oregonum*)
Harvest lily (*Brodiaea coronaria*)
Fool's onion (*Triteleia hyacinthina* or *Brodiaea hyacinthina*)
Hooker's onion (*Allium acuminatum*)
Rosy pussytoes (*Antennaria rosea* or *A. microphylla*)
Satin flower (*Sisyrinchium douglasii*)
Spring gold (*Lomatium utriculatum*)
Menzies' larkspur (*delphinium menziesii*)
Broad-leafed or Henderson's shootingstar (*Dodecatheon hendersonii*)
Grassland saxifrage (*Saxifraga integrifolia*)
Seablush (*Plectritis congesta*)
Few-flowered shootingstar (*Dodecatheon pulchellum*)
Wooly sunflower (*Eriophyllum lanatum*)
Early blue violet (*Viola adunca* var. *adunca*)

Rocky Outcrop & Slope Species
Idaho fescue or blue bunchgrass (*Festuca idahoensis*)
Broad-leafed stonecrop (*Sedum spathulifolium*)
Chickweek monkey-flower (*Mimulus alsinoides*)
Goldenback fern (*Pentagramma triangularis*)
Licorice fern (*Polypodium glycyrrhiza*)
Smooth alumroot (*Heuchera glabra*)
Spreading phlox (*Phlox diffusa*)
Spreading stonecrop (*Sedum divergens*)
Western saxifrage (*Saxifraga occidentalis*)
Woolly sunflower (*Eriophyllum lanatum*)

LISTED SPECIES (SELECTION)

Birds, Mammals & Reptiles
Northern pigmy owl (*Glaucidium gnoma swarthi*)
Western screech owl (*Megascops kennicottii kennicottii*)
Purple martin (*Progne subis*)
Horned lark (*Eremophila alpestris stringata*)
Peregrine falcon (*Falco peregrinus anatum*)
Vesper sparrow (*Pooecetes gramineus affinis*)
Western bluebird (*Sialia mexicanan* pop. 1)
Western meadowlark (*Sturnella neglecta* pop. 1)

Townsend's big-eared bat (*Corynorhinus townsendii*)
Ermine, Anguinae subspecies (*Mustela erminea anguinae*)
Sharp-tailed snake (*Contia tenuis*)

Plants

Farewell-to-spring (*Clarkia amoena* var. *caurina* and *lindleyi*)
White-top aster (*Sericocarpus rigidus*)
Deltoid balsamroot (*Balsamorhiza deltoidea*)
Golden paintbrush (*Castilleja levisecta*)
Victoria owl clover (*Castilleja victoriae*)
Macoun's meadowfoam (*Limnanthes macounii*)
Seaside bird's-foot lotus (*Lotus formosissimus*)
Bog bird's-foot trefoil (*Lotus Pinnatus*)
Dense-flowered lupine (*Lupinus oreganus var. kincaidii*)
Rosy owl clover (*Orthocarpus bracteosus*)
California buttercup (*Ranunculus californicus*)
Bear's-foot sanicle (*Sanicula arctopoides*)
Purple sanicle (*Sanicula bipinnatifida*)
Howell's triteleia (*Triteleia howellii*)
Yellow montane violet (*Viola praemorsa* ssp. *praemorsa*)

INVASIVE SPECIES

Plants

Scotch broom (*Cytisus scoparius*)
English ivy (*Hedera helix*)
Laurel-leaved daphne (*Daphne laureola*)
Common hawthorne (*Crataegus monogyna*)
Himalayan blackberry (*Rubus procerus*)
Gorse (*Ulex europaeus*)
Greater and common periwinkle (*Vinca major* and *minor*)
Poison-hemlock (*Conium maculatum*)
St. John's wort (*Hypericum perforatum*)
Carpet burweed (*Soliva sessilis*)
Orchard grass (*Dactylis glomerata*)
Canada thistle (*Cirsium arvense*)

Animals

House sparrow (*Passer domesticus*)
European starling (*Sturnus vulgaris*)
Eastern gray squirrel (*Sciurus carolinensis*)
Eastern cottontail rabbit (*Sylvilagus floridanus*)
Black slug (*Arion rufus*)

Bibliography

"A Pantheon of Trees", *Monday Magazine*, December 19, 2007, online issue.

Encyclopaedia Perthensis or Universal Dictionary of the Arts, Sciences Literature, etcetera, 2nd Edition. 1876.

American Bird Conservancy. *Media Release*, Washington, DC, August 11, 2011.

Arno, Stephen F. & Hammerly, Ramona P. *Northwest Trees*. The Mountaineers Books, 2007.

Benton, Fran. *One Less Orchid*. Independent Film Production, 2008.

Berkes, Fikret *et al.* "Rediscovery of Traditional Ecological Knowledge as Adaptive Management." *Ecological Applications*, 10(5) 2000, pp. 1251-1262.

Bjorkman, A. D. & Vellend, M. "Historical Baselines for Conservation: Ecological Changes Since European Settlement on Vancouver Island." *Conservation Biology*, 24, 1559-1568.

Bowman, David. "Does beauty really equal truth?" *Salon*, November 9, 1999. www.salon.com.

Boyd Michael. "Complete Rethink." *Wiener Zeitung*, March 2005.

Canadian Environmental Assessment Agency (CEAA). "Considering Traditional Ecological Knowledge," 2010. www.ceaa.gc.ca

Carlson, Keith Thor. *You Are Asked to Witness: The Sto:lo in Canada's Pacific Coast History*. Sto:lo Heritage Trust, 1997.

Cavers, Matthew Riddell. "Sub Quercu Felicitas: Place, Knowedge, and Victoria's Garry Oaks, 1843-2008". Queen's University (Thesis), 2008.

Clark, Ella E. *Indian Legends of the Pacific Northwest*. University of California Press, 1953.

Cleverly, Bill. "Environmentalists' report critical of Bear Mountain," *Times Colonist*, July 11, 2008.

Collinge, Sharon K. *Ecology of Fragmented Landscapes*. Johns Hopkins University Press, 2009.

Dagget, Dan. *Gardeners of Eden: Rediscovering Our Importance to Nature.* Thatcher Charitable Trust, 2005.

Devine, Warren & Harrington, Constance. "Garry Oak Woodland Restoration in the Puget Sound Region: Releasing Oaks from Overtopping Conifers and Establishing Oak Seedlings." 16th Int'l Conference, Society for Ecological Restoration, August 24-26, 2004, Victoria, Canada.

Dickens, Charles. *All the Year Round: A Weekly Journal.* London, 1866.

Douglas, David. *Journal Kept by David Douglas During His Travels in North America, 1823-1827.* William Wesley & Son, London, 1914.

Elms, Lindsay. *Beyond Nootka: A Historical Perspective of Vancouver Island Mountains.* Misthorn Press, 1996.

Fuchs, Marilyn A. *Towards a Recovery Strategy for Garry Oak and Associated Ecosystems in Canada: Ecological Assessment and Literature Review.* Technical Report GBEI/EC-00-030. Environment Canada, Canadian Wildlife Service, Pacific and Yukon Region, 2001.

Garry, Nicholas. *Diary of Nicholas Garry, Deputy-Governor of the Hudson's Bay Company from 1822-1835.* Royal Society of Canada, 1900.

Garry Oak Ecosystem Recovery Team. *The Garry Oak Gardener's Handbook: Nurturing Native Plant Habitat in Garry Oak Communities.* Victoria, 2009.

—— *Restoring British Columbia's Garry Oak Ecosystems: Principles and Practices.* Victoria, 2011.

Gottesfeld, Leslie M. Johnson. "The Importance of Bark Products in the Aboriginal Economies of Northwestern British Columbia, Canada." *Economic Botany*, Vol. 46, No. 2, 148-157.

Harbison, Robert. *Eccentric Spaces.* MIT Press, 2000.

Harrison, Robert Pogue. *Forests: The Shadow of Civilization.* University of Chicago Press, 1999.

—— *Gardens: An Essay on the Human Condition.* University of Chicago Press, 2008.

Harrington, Sheila & Stevenson, Judi. *Islands in the Salish Sea: A Community Atlas.* TouchWood Editions, 2005.

Hejinian, Lyn. *The Language of Inquiry.* University of California Press, 2000.

Hinchliffe, Steve. *Geographies of Nature: Societies, Environments, Ecologies.* Sage Publications, London, 2007.

Holland, John H. *Hidden Order: How Adaptation Builds Complexity.* Perseus Books, 1996.

Lea, Ted. "Historical Garry Oak Ecosystems of Vancouver Island, British Columbia, pre-European Contact to the Present." *Davidsonia* 17, 2006, 34-50.

Levin, Simon A. *Fragile Dominion: Complexity and the Commons.* Perseus Books, Massachusetts, 1999.

Lilburn, Tim. *Living In The World As If It Were Home: Essays.* Cormorant Books, 1999.

Luther, Kem. "An Ecosystem History." Slide presentation for the Victoria Natural History Association, 2011.

McKay, Don. *Apparatus.* McLelland & Stewart, 1997.

Mann, Charles C. "1491," *The Atlantic.* March 2002.

Maud, Ralph. *A Guide to BC Indian Myth and Legend*. Talonbooks, 1982.

Marshall, Daniel P. *Those Who Fell from the Sky*. Cowichan Tribes, 1999.

Mildon, Drew. Personal correspondence, 2011.

Minnis, Paul E & Elisens, Wayne J. *Biodiversity & Native America*. University of Oklahoma Press, 2000.

Pavord, Anna. *The Naming of Names: the Search for Order in the World of Plants*. Bloomsbury, 2005.

Parks Canada. "GO Restoration at Fort Rodd Hill," http://www.pc.gc.ca/eng/progs/np-pn/re-er/ec-cs/ec-cs05.aspx

Pettinger, April. *Native Plants in the Coastal Garden*. Whitecap Books, 2002.

Pojar & MacKinnon. *Plants of Coastal British Columbia*. Lone Pine Publishing, 1994.

Porteous, J. Douglas. *Landscapes of the Mind: Worlds of Sense and Metaphor*. University of Toronto Press, 1990.

Roemer, Hans Ludwig. "Forest Vegetation and Environments of the Saanich Peninsula, Vancouver Island". University of Victoria, 1972.

Scarry, Elaine. "Beauty and Social Justice". Keynote address, Pain in Performance and 'Moving Beauty.' Cambridge University, May 2010.

—— *On Beauty and Being Just*. Princeton University Press, 1999.

Sibley, David Allen. *The Sibley Field Guide to Birds of Western North America*. Knopf, New York, 2003.

Sultany, Molly L. *et al.* "Blue Flower of Tribal Legend: Skye blue petals resemble lakes of fine clear water." *Kalmiopsis*, vol. 14, 2007.

Taylor, Raymond L. *Plants of Colonial Days*. Dover Publications, New York, 1996

Turner, Nancy. *Food Plants of Coastal First Peoples*. Royal BC Museum, 1995.

—— *The Earth's Blanket: Traditional Teachings for Sustainable Living*. Douglas & McIntyre, 2005.

Turner, Nancy & Kuhnlein, Harriet V. "Camas (*Camassia* spp.) and Riceroot (*Fritillaria* spp.): Two Liliaceous 'Root' Foods of the Northwest Coast Indians." *Ecology of Food and Nutrition*, Vol 13, pp 199-219, 1983.

Turner, Nancy J. & Deur, Douglas, editors. *Keeping it Living: Traditions of Plant Use and Cultivation on the Northwest Coast of North America*. University of British Columbia Press, 2005.

Turner, Nancy J., *et al.* "Traditional Ecological Knowledge and Wisdom of Aboriginal Peoples in British Columbia." *Ecological Applications*, Vol 10, No. 5, pp. 1275-1287, 2000.

Weil, Simone. *Waiting for God*. Harper & Row, New York, 1951.

Zwicky, Jan. *Wisdom and Metaphor*. Gaspereau Press, 2003.

Acknowledgements

This book would not exist without those who supplied great quantities of generous, patient knowledge, on trails, boats and islands, in meadows, back gardens and nurseries. I wish to thank them for their dedication to Garry Oak ecosystems and the wonder they instill for all species. Thank you especially to Irvin Banman, Cecil Bannister, Adolf Ceska, Darren Copley, David Clements, Darren Copley, Butch Dick, Mike Ellerbeck, Tim Ennis, Matt Fairbarns, Kathleen Foley, Marilyn Fuchs, Clayton George, Chris Junck, Margaret Lidkea, Kem Luther, Roberta McCarthy, Terry McIntosh, Philip Marble, Carolyn Masson, Darcy Matthews, Kathryn Martell, Philip Kevin Paul, Adriane Pollard, Dave Polster, Kate Proctor, Betsy Rose, Ryan Senechal, Nancy Turner, Jody Watson, Jack Woodward and Rob at the Pacific Forestry Centre.

Thanks to Charles Campbell, for his attentive editing.

Thanks to Rolf Maurer for his belief in this project and to everyone at New Star Books for their care and dedication to publishing and design.

Thanks to Nick Russell for reading the earliest drafts and guiding me to hidden beauty; to Emrys Miller for his beautiful cover photos; to Jo Roueche for her art and to her and Sophie Wood for their gorgeous company during the year this book was written.

For accompaniment of heart, body and mind, Drew Mildon and Maisie the Dog.

NEW STAR BOOKS LTD.
107 – 3477 Commercial Street, Vancouver, BC V5N 4E8 CANADA
1574 Gulf Road, No. 1517, Point Roberts, WA 98281 USA
www.NewStarBooks.com   *info@NewStarBooks.com*

Cataloguing information for this title is available from Library and Archives Canada, http://www.collectionscanada.gc.ca/.

The publisher acknowledges the financial support of the Government of Canada through the Canada Council and the Department of Canadian Heritage Book Publishing Industry Development Program, and of the Province of British Columbia through the British Columbia Arts Council and the Book Publishing Tax Credit.

Cover by Mutasis.com
Cover photos by Emrys Miller
Map by Eric Leinberger
Typeset at New Star Books
Printed on 100% post-consumer recycled paper
Printed & bound in Canada by Gauvin Press
First printing, October 2012